EITHER
I WIN

GOD'S HOPE FOR
DIFFICULT TIMES

LOIS WALFRID JOHNSON

Augsburg Books

CONTENTS

To every person
who has suffered loss
and chooses
with the help of God
to win

PREFACE

DEAR FRIEND,

What does it mean to say, "Either way, I win"? How can you have hope even in the most difficult times of your life?

I was still a young mother when I faced a life-threatening diagnosis of cancer. Out of the knowledge that I might not live, I wrote the first edition of this book. If I didn't make it, there were things I wanted to say—words I wanted to leave behind.

Soon I discovered there are many forms of cancer. It's natural to think first of the kind seen under a microscope, but there are also cancers of fear, hurt, depression, loneliness, and unbelief. Cancers in which people face daily frustrations, no-win situations, suffering, and pain. Cancers of divorce or another loss of loved ones. Cancers that seem to end all hopes and dreams.

When things are going well, most of us plan our lives like a trip across the country. We study a map and set out, thinking that we'll arrive at our destination. We forget about detours—interruptions like a brief trip on a side road or interruptions so serious that they keep us from reaching our destination.

Centuries ago, Moses faced a life-changing interruption. As the adopted grandson of the Pharaoh of Egypt, Moses had every advantage. Growing up in a palace, he must have set his sights high and expected to do well. Instead he killed an Egyptian and fled to a foreign land. Forty years later, God spoke to Moses from a burning bush: "I'm sending you to Pharaoh to bring my people out of Egypt."

By then Moses had suffered enough to feel inadequate and afraid. "Who am I that I should go to Pharaoh?" he asked. "Who am I that I should bring the Israelites out of Egypt?" Out of his long years in the desert, Moses saw only the impossibilities of an extremely difficult assignment, not the opportunity of a lifetime.

But God didn't listen to his excuses. From the bush that burned without being destroyed, the Lord declared, "I AM WHO I AM. This is what you are to say to the Israelites: I AM has sent me to you" (Exod. 3:14 NIV).

By giving his name, God revealed his divine nature and character. In that one instant, a forty-year interruption became the foundation for a life's work. "It's not who *you* are," God told Moses. "What really counts is that I am *with* you."

In that time when I felt pushed against a wall by a life-threatening diagnosis of cancer, I knew that my life was not just interrupted. I could soon be *gone*—done with, over, *dead*. But when I cried out to the Lord, he graciously provided a door in the wall. In the moment he gave me the thought, "Either way, I win," everything changed. I knew that no matter what happened, I would win for one reason. Jesus Christ would be with me.

That was over twenty-three years ago. Since then, advances in diagnosis and treatment options for people who have breast cancer have markedly improved. There have also been significant improvements in the management and treatment of side effects related to cancer. I'll note some of those changes, but the spiritual concepts of dealing with something difficult remain the same.

In recent years, a number of people have talked to me about the original edition of *Either Way, I Win.* Some of them said, "Lois, you better update that book to tell people you are still alive. You need to prove that you did it." Each time I heard those words, I grieved. "Prove that *I* did it? You really think that *I* did it? That's the very worst reason for updating the book!"

Every year I've lived has been given to me. I can cooperate with the Lord, but he's the one who gives healing. And so, I'm back with this new edition, not because I've done all the "right" things and therefore am still alive. I know better. I'm back, not because I have "succeeded" in living where many others have died. Again, I know better. Instead I give you this updated book for one reason. Because of the ways in which I've been tested, I am even more certain that the God who said, "I am with you" *is* big enough.

Let me tell you why.

TROUBLE AHEAD

———◆●◆———

I hate to admit it,
but I'm scared, really scared.
My doctor says I need a biopsy.
What if it's the Big C?
Will you tell me what happened to you?

CANCER. ICE-LIKE, THE WORD BRINGS A CHILL. "Who has it? Which kind?"

This time it was my turn. When I discovered a lump between two ribs, my family doctor did not waste even a minute. While I was still in the examining room, he called a surgeon to make an appointment for the next afternoon.

At that consultation the surgeon explained a procedure often followed at that time. "We'll give you anesthetic for a biopsy and keep you under while we send the lump to the lab. If it's malignant—"

A cold feeling in the pit of my stomach told me the rest. If the lump were malignant, I might soon be facing a mastectomy, the surgery I dreaded most. Terrible as that would be, what might happen next? Would I be a cancer victim or a cancer survivor?

I could hope I would be among the large percentage of women who have a biopsy and learn they don't have cancer. Yet I believed otherwise. God had given me an inner certainty that my lump would be malignant. To my great surprise, I felt no panic, only the peace that I knew what was ahead and had faced the situation honestly.

In that dreadful moment more than twenty-three years ago, I discovered something. For most of my life I had believed that if I tried hard enough, I could succeed at almost anything. With the finding of one small lump, all that changed. Though I could still make some choices, my options would be limited. If there were cancer, I could not control what might happen, even to my own body.

During the brief period of time between that first appointment with the surgeon and the biopsy, I wanted time to talk with my family and closest friends. I asked two of these people, a Lutheran pastor and an Episcopal priest, to pray, anointing me with oil in the name of the Lord. As I knelt at the altar, one of them spoke in words remindful of Isaiah 43: "Fear not, I will take you through the waters."

I also needed time alone to think about the possibilities and somehow help myself feel better prepared if the news was bad. On the Friday before surgery, I drove out in the country and parked in a favorite spot. The day was unusually warm for a Minnesota spring, and in a quiet place I watched snow turn into rushing streams of water. Through my open car window, I felt the warmth of the sun and a gentle breeze. There I asked, "Lord, what do you want me to know?"

My question was born out of desperation. As a woman, even the sound of the word *mastectomy* frightened me. If I had to go through such a surgery, I didn't want to find out when surrounded by people.

And so, I took out my Bible. In my daily reading I had come to the twenty-second chapter of Luke. At first I could barely concentrate on what I was seeing. Then at verse 31, Christ's words to Peter seemed to fly off the page: "Simon, Simon, behold, Satan demanded to have you, that he might sift you like wheat."

Staring at the words, I thought, *It fits!* Not just because of a possible diagnosis of cancer. A multitude of difficult things had happened to our family that year. Already I felt as if I were being sifted like wheat. The warning doctors had given me about a mastectomy was going to be real. They weren't telling me the worst, just in case.

I could try to fool myself by hoping I would be among the countless women who have a routine biopsy. Yet the words of Jesus confirmed what I had sensed spiritually before seeing my doctor. Still, I felt no panic. Instead I prayed, "Lord, that's the surgery I dread most. Why, God? Why me?"

Then I saw Christ's promise to Peter: "But I have prayed for you that your faith may not fail." Immediately I asked, "Lord, will you pray for me, the way you prayed for Peter?"

As though Christ were speaking only to me, the rest of the promise seemed spotlighted. "When you have turned again, strengthen your brethren."

Turn again? What did that mean? I had no idea. *Strengthen my brothers and sisters in Christ?* I wondered, but only for a minute. Right then the other parts of the verse seemed more important—especially the part about being sifted. The reality of those words warned me about what was ahead. Much as I hoped otherwise, there was no doubt in my mind. It would be a mastectomy.

To my own great surprise, I did not feel the worry that often plagued my life. Only later did I experience the fear that nearly paralyzed me.

I used the Sunday I had before the biopsy as an opportunity to speak to my seventh-grade confirmation class. Several times I had talked to them about God's protection. "God offers you a resource for your everyday life," I had told them. "He wants you to ask for the power of his Spirit to help you cope with whatever you face."

Now I felt the need to say more about God's protection in every circumstance. "I want to be sure you understand that his protection comes in many different ways," I told them. "Sometimes we know his care for us through the peace and love he gives."

That afternoon, on Palm Sunday, I entered the hospital for the biopsy the next morning. Instead of the time that is often allowed now for considering surgical options, the decision about a mastectomy would be made while I was under anesthetic. If the biopsy proved malignant, the surgeon would do the mastectomy right away.

Deep within my heart there was a prayer: *Lord, don't allow me at any time to feel separated from your presence. If I lose my awareness of your love, I will have lost everything.*

Without realizing it, I had discovered the foundation of all our life principles:

> *When we fix our gaze on*
> *Jesus and keep it there, he*
> *gives us the faith we need.*

The next morning I woke early. The sleeping pill nurses had given me the night before had worn off, and they had not started to sedate me for surgery. Yet I was so filled with the Spirit's love, joy, and peace that I felt as if I were going to a party.

Wasn't I afraid? I had known fear before when waiting for even minor surgery. This time I faced the operation I most wanted to avoid. Yet Christ was with me. His presence washed over me, removing apprehension, giving peace as long as I was awake, and even when I woke up after my mastectomy.

In the recovery room I never asked, "What happened?" God had prepared me. I knew. Instead I wondered, *Did they get all the cancer? Is my husband okay?* Again, no fear, simply a wanting to know, and soon after, wanting to hear our daughter read God's words from Isaiah 43:1-3:

> *Fear not, for I have redeemed you;*
> *I have called you by name, you are mine.*
> *When you pass through the waters*
> *I will be with you;*
> *and through the rivers, they shall not*
> *overwhelm you. . . .*
> *For I am the Lord your God,*
> *the Holy One of Israel, your Savior.*

My family and I continued to know that sense of being carried in love. Two days after surgery, on the way back from my bath, I told the nurse who walked with me, "I really feel pretty good." But my thoughts added a footnote: *I wonder how I'll react when the final lab results come back.*

That afternoon I felt the support of countless prayers. I sensed Christ standing beside me when my surgeon said, "Lois, the pathology report shows cancer in six out of the eighteen lymph nodes we took from under your arm. You've had cancer for a long time."

Feeling as if I were a spectator watching someone else, I forced myself to ask, "How long do I have to live?"

"I don't know," the surgeon answered in that time before our present diagnostic tools. "I can't give you any amount of time."

I tried again, thinking he was afraid to tell me. "Christ is so real to me that I'm not afraid to die," I said. "But there's a book I'd like to write. Will I have enough time?"

He shook his head. "I can't tell you, Lois. When your incision has had time to heal, we'll start chemotherapy. You'll be on chemotherapy the rest of your life."

When my surgeon left the room, I was alone with my thoughts. They were not pleasant ones. Everything that lay ahead seemed bound by time—a lack of it. I had heard every word the doctor said and wasn't surprised. Though I often pushed the thought aside, I had felt unusually tired for several months. No matter what I needed to do, even the simplest tasks seemed overwhelming. More than that, God had prepared me spiritually for this diagnosis.

In my yearly checkup only two months before, I had received a clean bill of health. Now I felt relieved that I had found the lump in a routine breast exam. Because of its position between two ribs, I must have missed the tumor for some time.

Now questions flew at me like pieces of broken glass. *What about my husband? He's already lost one wife through illness and death. If I die, what will happen to him? What will happen to our children?*

Soon visitors would fill my room. In those moments before the well-meaning invasion began, I asked more frightening questions: "Lord, what's going to happen to me? What do you want me to know? Do I need to prepare my husband and children for my death? Or will you allow me to live?"

————◆◆————

FAITH THOUGHT

AND MY GOD WILL SUPPLY EVERY NEED OF YOURS ACCORDING TO HIS RICHES IN GLORY IN CHRIST JESUS. (PHIL. 4:19)

Lord Jesus,
in the moment of bad news,
in that time of fear and anxiety,
I need that still small space
in which I know without doubt
that you care about everything
that happens to me.
You see my difficult circumstances.
You understand how I feel.
Though I'm scared to ask,
will you tell me what I need to know?
Will you help me in a way so clear
that I cannot misunderstand?

Thank you that in the moment of crisis,
in the shock and numbness of disbelief,
you are with me.
Thank you that you hold, and strengthen,
and cradle me like an infant
within your protecting arms.

WALK OUT OF FEAR

———◆●◆———

When I look at the impossibilities
I have all I can do not to panic
about what lies ahead.
How can I cope with my fear
of the unknown?

I N THE DAYS FOLLOWING SURGERY, I discovered that the people
who visited me in the hospital had already dealt with their
feelings about cancer. They had gone beyond their fears in order
to encourage me. But when I returned home, I quickly learned I
had to face another question. How should I cope with a fear of the
unknown that could overwhelm my strongest beliefs?

"Fear not," God had said in Isaiah 43:1. I needed his words the
first time I entered a large room filled with people. I knew most of
them. They had heard about my medical condition, and it wasn't
hard to read their faces. They looked at me, then away, as though
hoping they wouldn't have to talk with me.

Their expressions told me they were afraid of cancer. In those
years before open conversations about cancer, they didn't know
what to do or say to me, so they said nothing. As far as I was concerned, I had only begun the fight for my health. Yet the fear they
showed in my presence gave me a signal: *For them I'm already dead.*

Before long, I encountered something even more difficult.
Because of all that had happened to me, I longed to hear people
say, "I'm sorry to hear that you've had surgery, but you look

strong now." Or, "I understand you were diagnosed with cancer. I'll be praying for you." Instead someone usually said, "Sorry to hear you've been in the hospital. How are you doing?" Before I could answer, the well-wisher rushed on: "You know, my brother had cancer, and . . ."

Had, I thought. *And he didn't live.*

None of the stories were about a person who survived. Whoever the patient was, his struggle was long and difficult, ultimately ending in death. I soon felt like a pedestrian hit by a semi filled with bad news. With the seventh or eighth story I felt overwhelmed. Then fear set in: *What if all that awful stuff happens to me?* It didn't make any difference that I couldn't possibly experience what ten people had.

With my mind I tried to forgive the people involved. *They don't realize how sensitive I am right now.* But it was harder to deal with my emotions. *How many people die of cancer? How many people die of fear?*

Only once in those early weeks did someone say, "My mother had a bout with cancer, and some of her friends have also. Mom has positive feelings about your situation."

"Courage is not the absence of fear," said Captain Eugene McDaniel in a radio interview following his Vietnamese prisoner-of-war experience. "Courage is the presence of faith." If courage is the presence of faith, how could I grow in my faith? How could I have a faith strong enough to counteract my fear?

I soon learned that coming to a greater faith, an in-spite-of-fear kind of faith, was not something I could accomplish by myself. God is the giver of faith. But he would give me what I needed only if I allowed him. Because I had no choice but to seek his help, I discovered another life principle:

> *Fear can make us a prisoner or*
> *give us a reason to grow. Faith in*
> *Christ takes us beyond our strongest fear.*

When I told the Lord I wanted to grow, he started me on a process in which I asked four questions that have helped me in every time of testing since.

1) Have I faced what is happening to me?

Cancer patients quickly learn the meaning of the word *metastasis*. It's a process in which malignant cells break away and spread to other parts of the body, forming new tumors. Fear metastasizes the same way, taking over our thoughts and emotions, spreading to every part of the body.

Fear thrives on the unknowns and takes over when I lose balance in the way I see things. My reactions build up, often out of proportion to the trouble I face. By pushing aside and refusing to deal with the reasons I'm afraid, I encourage fear to metastasize. As an oncology nurse said, "We can't do anything to help cancer patients until they face the fact that they have cancer."

When my surgeon gave me a life-threatening diagnosis, I had to choose how I would react. Should I pretend I didn't hear what he said? Should I block it out of my mind? Or should I be honest about the possibilities and ask, "What will happen to me?"

In every form of suffering, this question is one of the most crucial and frightening. Asking it means that we understand we're close to the edge of a cliff. We don't know any way to keep from falling off. Yet as I faced cancer, I discovered that I had the best possible answer to that scary question, "What will happen to me?" I knew without doubt that I was a Christian. Even if the worst happened, I would receive eternal life.

Previously I had faced death many times, or so I thought. But on each occasion I had faced the death of someone I loved— not my own. My feelings about life-threatening illness were interwoven with my awareness of how much I'd miss the person who died. Always the ache of loneliness interfered with my view of the resurrection. It came as a release to realize that the idea of losing someone I love is more threatening than the idea of losing my own life.

I remembered the process I went through before surgery. *Am I ready to die?* I asked myself. My answer was immediate: *Yes, I am. Jesus Christ is my Lord and Savior.*

Am I afraid to die? I wondered next. I didn't relish the pain that might precede death. But often I had seen death as a liberation from pain. My concern was for those who loved me. They would know the loneliness. I wouldn't.

Out of that knowledge I became aware of how real Christ is for me. The words of the apostle Paul seemed to jump off the page: "None of us lives for himself only, none of us dies for himself only. If we live, it is for the Lord that we live, and if we die, it is for the Lord that we die. So whether we live or die, we belong to the Lord" (Rom. 14:7-8 TEV). As I stared at those words I realized I would win, either way.

"Either way, I win" became my special thought from the Lord, the encouragement that carried me through difficult hours, weeks, months, and years.

In every kind of testing there's an important truth. In the moment we admit our difficulty to the Lord, we give him the opportunity to help. And so, I needed to ask another question.

2) Where do I look for help?

As I met people in whom I saw a fear of cancer, it was as though I heard God's gentle whisper: "Fear not. I will take you through the waters." Yet I had to decide where I would look. At the waters—my fear of all that might happen? At myself and my inability to control all that was happening? Or should I look to God? I could ask him to help me cope with the fear instilled by what I heard. I could ask him to lead me through the unknowns that lay ahead.

When I chose to look to God, he seemed to say, "Turn the stories over to me. Give me every fear. Ask for a hedge of protection around yourself, your husband, your children. Through my Son I saved you from eternal death. I also want to save you from living in fear."

Again I recalled the words God spoke through Isaiah: "Fear not . . . I have called you by name, you are mine." I asked for the hedge of protection that surrounded Job when Satan wanted to test him (Job 1:10). Though I still heard the stories, they didn't have the same power to frighten me.

3) Do I pray the moment I feel afraid?

It's easy to use prayer as a last resort, instead of a first resource. When I release my problems to God, I give him permission to deal with them.

In his book *Prayer*, O. Hallesby writes, "Prayer and helplessness are inseparable. Only he who is helpless can truly pray. . . . Your helplessness is your best prayer. . . . To pray is nothing more involved than to open the door, giving Jesus access to our needs and permitting Him to exercise His own power in dealing with them."

In daily life I'm a good door opener. I pass from one room to another or from my home into a friend's. I open a car door, wanting to go somewhere, or a refrigerator door, planning to eat. That same ability is important in my spiritual life, but I may need Hallesby's reminder: "To pray is to open the door unto Jesus. And that requires no strength. It is only a question of our wills."

As I use my will to tell God my needs, I discover I can be totally honest. God already knows the worst about me. I don't have to pretend I'm something I'm not. Often I pray, "Lord, I'm afraid. I give that anxiety to you." As I relinquish whatever I'm feeling, God begins working in me. Sometimes he gives me an insight that tells me what to do. On other occasions he encourages my faith, giving me the ability to trust him for the long view. In still other ways God seems to whisper, "You need to talk with someone, Lois." Prayer was never intended as an escape from working out issues or problems that need to be talked about with those closest to us. Neither is prayer an excuse for avoiding responsibility.

In the process of walking out of fear, I came to another question.

4) Do I let God carry the weight? Have I left my fears with him?

More than once I needed to ask myself, "Is this something God expects me to handle, or is it his responsibility?" If I tell God my needs but continue to muddle around in them, I don't enter the peace he promises. Instead I fall into unbelief. Through my anxiety I tell God that he is unable to take care of a situation.

I discovered that it's more difficult to worry about something that *might* happen than to face that problem when it's real. Much as I disliked having a mastectomy, there was something freeing about it. The surgery I had dreaded most wasn't as bad as I assumed it would be.

After I turn a situation over to God, it's important that I don't take it back again. Think about packing a suitcase. One by one, I put in each difficulty and reason for fear, then close the suitcase. I carry it to the foot of the cross, put it down at the feet of Jesus, and say, "It's all yours, Lord." When fear returns, I pray, "Lord, I've left that with you. Don't allow me to pick up that suitcase again."

In his play *Julius Caesar,* Shakespeare put it well: "Cowards die many times before their deaths; the valiant never taste of death but once." We can be valiant only when we truly leave our fears with God. In the midst of intense emotions and reasons for fear coming from every direction, how can we learn a steady walk of trust in him?

FAITH THOUGHT

"HAVE I NOT COMMANDED YOU? BE STRONG AND OF GOOD COURAGE; BE NOT FRIGHTENED, NEITHER BE DISMAYED; FOR THE LORD YOUR GOD IS WITH YOU WHEREVER YOU GO." (JOSH. 1:9)

When I fear the unknowns—
the trials that come to all people,
the tests that are part
of being alive—
remind me, Lord,
that you provide the ability
to run the race of life.
I turn over to you
each one of my fears.
In the mighty name of Jesus
I ask for protection
for my loved ones and me.
Thank you for giving me
the ability to endure and faith
in spite of circumstances.
In faith I receive your help,
your peace, your crown of victory!

CHAPTER THREE

STANDING UP WHEN FEELING DOWN

———◆●◆———

*Sometimes day-to-day living
seems harder than facing a crisis.
How can I be an overcomer,
even in the everydays?*

O N A SUMMER VACATION, our family visited Colorado's famous Royal Gorge. Far above the Arkansas River, we walked across the world's highest suspension bridge. Over one thousand feet beneath us, the cola-tinted water snaked its way between sheer cliffs, splashing white against huge boulders. As I looked down, I wondered, *How strong is the bridge holding us up?*

Glancing around, I saw countless small wires bound into two large cables. Extending from one side to the other, those cables spanned the chasm, providing support for the planks on which we stood.

During the weeks after surgery, I often felt that I stood high above such a chasm. God never promised that as a Christian I would live without problems. Yet because I seek God, I find greater resources for dealing with whatever chasm I face.

Like a suspension bridge, God's support for us is held by two special cables—the opportunity to turn to Scripture and the privilege of knowing God through prayer. As I used those cables, I needed to be honest with the Lord about what was happening to me. I had to start where I was in my present level of spiritual growth and allow him to lead me on. I especially needed to learn how to focus on Christ, instead of my circumstances.

In Philippians 4:8-9 Paul writes, "Finally, brethren, whatever is true, whatever is honorable, whatever is just, whatever is pure, whatever is lovely, whatever is gracious, if there is any excellence, if there is anything worthy of praise, think about these things. What you have learned and received and heard and seen in me, do; and the God of peace will be with you."

Paul doesn't say, "Avoid thinking about the things you want to deny." Instead he tells us, "Choose what you're going to concentrate on so that the God of peace will be with you."

After I received the diagnosis of cancer, my friend and former editor, Ron Klug, wrote from Madagascar to ask, "Lois, I'd be curious to know what you're reading nowadays."

"The Bible," I wrote back. "Only the Bible is big enough."

For as long as I can remember I've enjoyed daily Bible reading. For my time with the Lord I try to find a place where I'm alone. I like to come to him in the morning, so that whatever I learn helps me the rest of the day.

Usually I start with praise and worship. In order to hear from God, it's important that I have an open and prepared spirit. Psalm 100:4 tells us, "Enter his gates with thanksgiving, and his courts with praise! Give thanks to him, bless his name!"

As I move from songs of praise into worship, I tell the Lord that I love and appreciate him. By singing hymns and spiritual songs, I set aside distractions and focus my attention on the Lord. Then I ask forgiveness for my sins and allow the Holy Spirit to prepare my spirit for what he wants to say to me.

I vary what I do in my devotional time, but it always centers around a portion of Scripture—usually a chapter or two a day.

Sometimes I follow a program in which I read through the Bible in one year. Other times I read until I receive the help I need and stop there to think about a verse and pray it through. After reading Scripture, it's important to be still and write down what God says through his inspired Word. I also like to read a daily selection from a devotional classic such as *My Utmost for His Highest* by Oswald Chambers.

My daily oasis of time with God was helpful to me as I struggled with whatever I faced. As I chose to concentrate on the Lord and what he wanted me to know, I took hold of a cable that reached—something that helped me, no matter what my circumstances. In those months after surgery, I discovered a four-step process that has helped me ever since: find, take hold, pray and affirm, and then kneel on the promise.

1) Find the promise.

No two things can occupy the same place at the same time. When I need guidance, or if fear and other negative thoughts threaten, I tell God my specific need. Usually I put it down in writing so that I'm clear about my concern. I ask the Lord to open my heart and spirit, and I pray, "Lord, what do you want me to know?" As I read my Bible, I notice what verse or verses speak to that concern.

Often someone asks me, "How do you get an answer from God? Do you know where to turn and just look for that verse?" At times I do need certain passages of reassurance and turn to favorites. Yet as a regular Bible reader, I usually just start reading wherever I left off. It always delights me to see how the Lord manages to give me exactly the verse or passage I need on the day I need it.

I pay special attention to any verse or verses that seem to be lit by God's holy spotlight. In a *Guideposts* article, John Sherrill describes what that means:

> For a long time I had been aware of a strange phenomenon. The Bible had an amazing way of speaking to current situations in my life. As I read it each morning, one particular verse always

seemed to stand out from the page, a new verse for each day. It was as if the passage was illuminated by a kind of spiritual spotlight, highlighted to draw attention to it.

In questioning whether those illuminated verses fall into a special category, Sherrill asked, "Could they be daily gifts from God, mystically designed *to be used that very same day?*" Like Sherrill, I have found they often are. Verses or passages God wants me to notice seem to jump off the page.

I find that in an amazing way the key thought in the chapter of Scripture often corresponds with the verse my devotional book suggests. That agreement confirms in my mind and spirit the message I believe the Lord wants me to know.

I underline such verses in my Bible. I write them into my prayer journal and copy them onto three-by-five cards so I can memorize or return to them often. On the back side of those cards I write the date and the reason that verse spoke to me. Months or years later I come back to those cards, journal entries, and underlined verses, and see how God has worked in my life. His attention to even small details reminds me that he cares for me as a person.

During the weeks following surgery, I often thought about our twenty-two-year-old daughter, who had been born during my husband's first marriage. Two and a half years old when her mother died, Gail was four and a half when we married. Now, because of the involvement in my lymph nodes, I wondered, *Will Gail be losing yet another mother?*

Then one day, as I walked through a parking lot, I looked up at our nearly six-foot-tall fifteen-year-old. I asked myself, *Will I live long enough to see him happily married? And what about our thirteen-year-old? Will he become a well-balanced, mature adult if I'm not around?*

I had no doubt that God could do all kinds of amazing miracles in their lives, even without my help. At the same time, I truly wanted to be a mother for them in their growing-up years. Out of that I prayed, "Lord, what do you want me to know about my children?"

The morning after I asked that question, I received an answer during my daily Bible reading. With his holy spotlight the Spirit called my attention to Paul's words in Philippians 1:6: "And I am sure that he who began a good work in you will bring it to completion at the day of Jesus Christ."

The promise struck home. I thought, *That's for me!* I believe God began a good work in me when Gail became my daughter through marriage. He began another good work in the moments in which our sons were conceived. Whether I lived or died, the Lord would bring to completion the work begun in my children. Either way, I would win, and so would they.

2) Take hold of the promise.

When the Holy Spirit illuminates a verse, I believe those words are a personal message to me. Because the Christ who "is the same yesterday and today and for ever" (Heb. 13:8) still lives, I respond in faith, thanking the Lord.

As his Spirit breathes life into promises, he gives the certainty that he truly is speaking to me. That certainty does not come because I try to manipulate God or twist Scripture to say what I want. Instead I'm like a starving person who needs bread. My certainty develops out of regular Bible reading and openness to *whatever* God tells me, whether I need to ask forgiveness or celebrate joy, prepare for death, or struggle to live.

By taking hold of a promise, I take God at his word. I believe that the promise he has made real is what he wants me to know.

When I received the diagnosis of cancer, I was in the midst of a seminary course. Our professor, Dr. Mark Hillmer, had asked us to read aloud and tape the Psalms. I had partially completed this work when I checked into the hospital for a biopsy. After surgery, I used an earplug to listen to those tapes without bothering my roommate. I experienced in a new way how the Spirit brings to life what he wants us to hear. Before surgery, he had used certain psalms to convict me of areas in which I was resentful or needed to forgive. During hospitalization the identical passages offered consistent comfort.

In every aspect of my life, I want to establish a pattern of taking God at his word. There's a life principle involved:

> *Though our need is great, our*
> *resources in Christ are even greater.*

The Bible is God's inspired Word to encourage, guide, and strengthen us, as well as show us how to live. The seemingly small action of saying in faith, "That Bible verse is for me!" begins a chain of events in which we allow ourselves to be excited about what God can do.

3) Pray and affirm the promise.

I invite God to increase my faith by praying the Bible verses his Spirit has highlighted. With Philippians 1:6 I prayed, "Lord, you have said you will bring to completion a good work begun in me. I believe your promise. In the name of Jesus, I ask that you bring all three of our children to mature Christian adulthood. Thank you for caring about their needs in the years ahead."

Through God's grace, I have lived long enough to see him answer that prayer. That does not mean that every day of parenting has been easy. Yet step-by-step our children have reached a place of faith in the Lord. Each of them now have families of their own, and their lives are full, rich, and God-blessed.

Praying the promise is not the same as positive thinking where a person chooses what thought he or she wishes to concentrate on and repeats it over and over. Instead we pray the verse that God out of his sovereign knowledge of our situation has made real to us. Such verses have a power that no other words have. We receive and pray verses in a way that is consistent with the overall teachings of Scripture.

In John 15:16 Christ reminds us of the importance of praying in his name: "You did not choose me, but I chose you and appointed you that you should go and bear fruit and that your fruit should abide; so that whatever you ask the Father in my name, he may give it to you." Asking in Christ's name seems a small "wire," but it's part of an exceedingly strong cable. So, too, are Paul's words in Philippians 4:6: "Have no anxiety about anything, but in everything by prayer and supplication with thanksgiving let your requests be made known to God."

If I fail to see answers to prayer, I ask myself, *Did I thank God?* I've known persons who interceded for years for the salvation of loved ones without seeing an answer until they prayed, "Thank you for their salvation." *With thanksgiving* suggests thanking the Lord the moment I ask, before receiving an answer. Paul didn't say, "Wait ten years until you get the results." It's tempting to think, *Well, maybe God will answer, but I'm not really sure, so I'm not going to thank him until I know.* I need to thank the Lord again when I see the answer, but thanking immediately affirms my belief that he *will* act.

Someone who prayed with me once asked, "Lois, how can you say thank you before you see the answer?" After thinking a moment I told her, "Often I thank the Lord out of the knowledge of past experiences, knowing that he will perform his work because he is faithful. At other times I thank him out of trust, because of what he promises."

From experiences of wondering if the cables will reach, I've learned that thanking God immediately is a powerful way to pray. One morning I interceded for a friend whose need was so big it seemed totally hopeless. I felt as if I had no faith, yet out of habit I added, "Thank you, Lord, that you're working already, even though I can't see it." Within an hour I received a phone call. The friend told me, "Lois, you won't believe what happened!" God had answered my prayer for her situation.

While I often feel lacking in faith, I don't want to swing to the opposite extreme—having faith in faith. When I pray promises he spotlights, I simply believe God's word to me and use it as a guideline for prayer. My faith is in God, not in what I do.

God doesn't expect me to always come on the peak of faith, believing 100 percent of the way. In *Appointment with God* Alvin Rogness writes, "When these thoughts come, as they do, I simply say to God, 'You'll have to take me as I am, doubts and all.'" Faith, as Dr. Rogness points out, is a gift from the Holy Spirit. Yet each one of us makes a choice whether to pray or not to pray. When we lack faith, it helps to pray the promises the Holy Spirit has made real. It also helps to understand that whether we praise, worship, or pray, we choose to do so with our will.

If I bury whatever faith I do have, it doesn't grow but rots in the ground. Yet when I use my will to express even a microscopic amount of faith, I allow the Holy Spirit to give me more. I won't run out; he'll fill me again. My part is being honest with God.

4) Kneel on the promise.

There's an old hymn about standing on the promises. More than once, I found myself unable to stand. At times only a few hours passed before I needed to go back to the verse given that morning. As I read it aloud, I felt as if the promise were a cement slab. I was not standing, but kneeling on that cement, clutching its corners with my fingers.

To stand or kneel on a promise means to rest in what it says. It means continuing to believe what God has promised, in spite of fear that says the contrary. The powers of darkness prefer to have us lukewarm or discouraged, instead of victorious. When doubts invade me, I repeat my promise for that day. I pray, "Lord, this is your promise. I believe it," for as long as necessary to come to peace.

Before surgery, the Lord used the first part of Luke 22:31-32 to help me. During my eighteen months on chemotherapy, the last part of that verse returned to me often: "And when you have turned again, strengthen your brethren."

At first I wondered what that strengthening of others would involve. I remembered those words as I bargained, "Lord, you've been training me as a writer. Aren't you going to allow me time to work?" I recalled those words as I thought, *I'm glad for every writers' conference at which I've taught. I'm thankful for each time I've helped Christians learn to write. They can continue if I can't.* Always the word *time* crept into my thoughts. *How much time did I have?*

Seventeen days after surgery I returned to the hospital for further tests, because my doctor wondered if cancer had spread to my bones. The process of having a bone scan and mammogram, then visiting his office, took most of the day. I returned home exhausted and crawled into bed, certain that the tests would reveal bad news.

Then I opened a devotional book. The verses suggested for the day concerned Abraham:

> He did not weaken in faith when he considered his own body, which was as good as dead because he was about a hundred years old, or when he considered the barrenness of Sarah's womb. No distrust made him waver concerning the promise of God, but he grew strong in his faith as he gave glory to God, fully convinced that God was able to do what he had promised. (Rom. 4:19-21)

As I read those words, my discouragement changed to hope. I sensed that my test results would be all right. When I called my doctor's office the next morning, I found that to my great relief they were.

Living without fear or anxiety is not something any one of us can learn overnight. Even now, twenty-three years after surgery, I know it is a process. On the day I think I've learned something, I slip backward again. In those moments I try to remember it is God's action, his moving ahead, and my willingness to work with him that bring a change.

Because of the time period in which I was diagnosed and because of the involvement in my lymph nodes, doctors told me I could not consider myself healed unless I lived for twenty years. That kind of prognosis is now somewhat different. Yet I felt sure that God did not want me living in fear for whatever time I had left. I believed he wanted to give me his courage so I could value each day as the gift that it is.

In my life of faith it's important to kneel on promises the Holy Spirit has made real to me personally. Those promises come from the God "who never lies" (Titus 1:2; see also Heb. 6:18). Tiny wires, some of them, yet bound together into the strong cable of his Word. That cable, coupled with the cable of prayer, bridges whatever chasms I face, for as I look across I see Christ standing with outstretched arms on the other side.

Faith Thought

"WHEN THE SPIRIT OF TRUTH COMES, HE WILL GUIDE YOU INTO ALL THE TRUTH; FOR HE WILL NOT SPEAK ON HIS OWN AUTHORITY, BUT WHATEVER HE HEARS HE WILL SPEAK, AND HE WILL DECLARE TO YOU THE THINGS THAT ARE TO COME. HE WILL GLORIFY ME, FOR HE WILL TAKE WHAT IS MINE AND DECLARE IT TO YOU." (JOHN 16:13-14)

Bread.
I desperately need it, Lord.
I need you, the Living Bread,
and the water that will not run dry.
I praise you, Holy Spirit,
for the warm sense
of being taught by you.
Thank you for the moments
when you bring God's message alive,
as though it were written
or spoken only for me.
Thank you that when I turn
your promises into prayers
your Word becomes flesh
and dwells within me.
Give me boldness
in repeating your promises
until your words
become mine through faith.

FREE TO LIVE!

―◆●◆―

"I think I'm going to make it,"
the cancer patient said.
"But how can I be sure
that I'll win,
no matter what happens?"

DURING THE SUMMER I WAS THREE YEARS OLD, my family and I spent our vacation at a cabin loaned to us. To the concern of my parents, the beach fell away rapidly. Near the end of the dock the water was over my head. My six-year-old sister, Faith, my two-year-old sister, Ruth, and I heard repeated warnings: "Don't go out on the dock!"

One morning while Dad was fishing, Mom took my younger sister to the cabin. Though they were gone for just a few minutes, I walked out on the dock. Of course, I fell in.

Panic washed over me as I tried to touch bottom and couldn't. Sunlight streamed through the water, but I felt myself turning in somersaults. As pressure built up in my ears, I struggled for air. Then I felt a hand clutch my arm.

The hand tugged hard, dragging me from the water. My older sister had jumped in. Just tall enough to stand on the bottom, Faith pulled me onto the beach.

Years later my parents told me, "Lois, if you had struggled, you would have been too much for her. She couldn't have dragged you in. Because you allowed her to pull you out, Faith saved you."

In my spiritual struggle, that is grace: being saved from drowning, not by anything I do, but by faith. Because of grace, I was able to face cancer and say, "Either way, I win." As Paul writes: "For by grace you have been saved through faith; and this is not your own doing, it is the gift of God—not because of works, lest any man should boast" (Eph. 2:8-9).

I could have thrashed around, saying in effect, "I'll do everything myself. I'll handle my frustrations. I'll take care of my fears, whether the cancer is physical, emotional, or spiritual. I'll even cope with my fears about death." But I would have made matters worse.

During visits to my oncologist, or cancer specialist, I met a sixty-four-year-old man whose tumor was inside his rib cage, next to his heart, and therefore inoperable. Yet the tumor was treatable with chemotherapy and radiation. As it diminished in size, the man returned to his pre-cancer weight. In a gruff voice he expressed his hope: "I think I'm going to make it."

"I hope I will too," I answered. "But if not, I'm ready to die."

Instantly I realized I had made him uncomfortable. I was not surprised when he changed the subject. Just the same, on subsequent visits when our medical appointments coincided, the man remained friendly, initiating conversation. I could almost feel him thinking, *I better keep in contact with that lady. She knows how to help—just in case.* But no matter how I tried to talk about an honest preparation for death, he always edged away from the topic.

His situation is not unique. Countless people seem to believe that if they don't think about cancer, let alone talk about it, they will escape both cancer and death. With each person who feels that way, I've wanted to pass on Joseph Bayly's words in his book *View from a Hearse*: "The paradox is that when you accept the fact of death, you are freed to live."

When my surgeon and I discussed how cancer was present in six out of the eighteen lymph nodes, he said, "You've had cancer for some time." As I thought about his words, I faced the reality of my position. I asked myself, *What would be the worst that could happen?* Out of that grew concern for my family.

About the same time, I developed resentment toward people who assumed I was already dead or would die in the next breath, even though I looked good and had resumed normal activities. *Treat me as though I'm still alive!* I thought. Yet it didn't take long to realize I was free in a way they were not. I was not trying to hide from the inevitability that touches every person. I had faced the possibility of death and knew peace in spite of circumstances. That peace found in Christ saved me from drowning, for I had discovered a life principle:

> *When we're ready to*
> *die, we are free to live.*
> *Either way, we win!*

In the biggest moments of life each of us stands alone. Yet God offers a resource bigger than aloneness. He wants us to have assurance, to know without doubt that we are ready for now and for eternity. Jesus does not want anyone to be a slave, bound by whatever or whoever demands attention. Those feeling most lost have the deepest need of him. "Admit honestly to me who you are and where you have been," he says with his life. "I love you. You don't have to make yourself over before becoming my friend."

Because of that unconditional love, I have the privilege of knowing an understanding Lord who accepts me in whatever condition I come. Then, *if I allow him*, he draws my gaze from my incompleteness. As a divine Savior, he forgives and changes me into what I would like to become.

Many pitied me because I had cancer. Yet through illness I discovered that God frees me to live and be a winning person, no matter what the circumstances. Christian counselors agree, "The gospel is an invitation to celebrate wholeness." By being able to answer the question, "Am I ready to die?" I was ready to live and celebrate wholeness in spite of a mastectomy. An insightful Jewish woman summed it up: "I know the difference between Christians. Some believe in religion or in the activities of their church. Others believe in Christ."

Through his death on the cross Jesus offers the opportunity for every one of us to be forgiven. But how did I *know* without doubt that I was ready to die?

Years before, I had been born into a Christian home. Each day my father led us in reading from the Bible. From my earliest remembrance, my mother taught us to pray. I can't remember a time when I did not love the Lord.

As a Lutheran pastor, my father had developed an unusually good confirmation program— a combination of Bible history, catechism, and in-depth study of such books of the Bible as John and Acts. I liked learning a key verse in each of those two books because the truths were so helpful to me. On confirmation day I made public confession of my faith and meant every word of it. Yet less than six months later, at the time when many young people drop out of church, I started questioning what I believed. I wondered, *Do I believe all these things for myself? Or do I believe them because of what my parents say?*

After making my public confession of faith, I was embarrassed to admit that I had doubts. I thought that if Jesus were my Lord, he would want me to do something I really wouldn't want to do. I feared that he might even turn me into some kind of Jesus freak. I failed to recognize that Christ's love is always present: "There is no fear in love, but perfect love casts out fear" (1 John 4:18a).

While thinking I didn't know if I could trust God to give me something good, I needed to understand that God works in a way that is consistent with our personality. He retains our identity, but adds strength and joy. As Lee Evenson says, "He wants to add life to our days, not just days to our life."

The joy of Christ is a serenity of spirit *in spite of circumstances*. I have seen that joy even in seriously ill cancer patients. Nurses brought an African American woman to a hospital support group in a wheelchair. Before a roomful of people she began singing in the melodic strains of her people. The group grew quiet, listening attentively as with a radiant face she told how God had filled her with his love that morning.

That joy and knowledge of being loved is available to every-one. As a questioning teenager, I didn't tell anyone I was search-ing. Instead I listened. Without knowing my need, my dad faithfully taught what the Bible says about salvation. He made the biblical plan of salvation so clear that I could not miss it. In his Sunday-by-Sunday preaching, he used crucial verses and showed me how to put them together. It was not with what Paul calls "high-sounding words" that I came to the assurance of what I believed. It was through my father's use of Scripture.

Romans 3:23 became real to me: "All have sinned and fall short of the glory of God." I could not shake off Romans 3:10-12: "None is righteous, no, not one; no one understands, no one seeks for God. All have turned aside, together they have gone wrong; no one does good, not even one."

Yet there is hope! "But God shows his love for us in that while we were yet sinners Christ died for us" (Rom. 5:8). The free gift of God is salvation through the death of his Son, Christ Jesus, on the cross. That death was for the sins of all people, including me.

When I struggled with the meaning of that cross, it was not because Jesus made the experience of personal salvation some-thing difficult. I struggled because God gives freedom of choice. He could have said, "I'm going to create you so you have no choice but to love me." Instead he gave each of us free will. That will gives us the freedom to decide for or against a God who seeks in love to draw us to himself.

Some in danger of drowning object, "I wasn't interested in God when I was well," or, "I need him now because I'm over-whelmed by problems. But isn't it terrible to want God because I'm desperate?" Certainly it's better to establish a relationship with God when things are going well. Those who do have the advantage of learning how big his resources are through experience. But many people put off receiving the power that is available to them. If problems or chronic illness becomes the means by which a rela-tionship with Christ comes alive, suffering is not wasted.

In *Mere Christianity*, C. S. Lewis says, "When you are arguing against God you are arguing against the very power that makes you able to argue at all." As my friend Jan puts it, "Faith will not be victorious until we stop fighting ourselves and surrender to the inevitability of God's love."

It's tempting to let pride get in the way of the most important choice we ever make. It's tempting to feel we can somehow make it on our own. I came to Jesus by receiving his promises. In John 14:6 he says, "I am the way, and the truth, and the life; no one comes to the Father, but by me." At times that one way sounds too simple. We may feel we need to work even to achieve eternal life. Instead being set free means coming as a little child to accept Christ's open arms. After reading my first book, *Just a Minute, Lord,* thirteen-year-old Cathy Hillmer made a banner for me. Against a circle of multicolored felt pieces lies a black cross. Above it are words that remind us of the significance of Christ's death: "Thanks for taking my place."

Yes, too easy; yet sometimes too difficult.

It can also be tempting to think that I have plenty of time to make a choice. As I continued going for chemotherapy, I always looked for the man with a tumor near his heart. I never had the privilege of telling him how to make his peace with the Lord. I've often wondered whether he lived or died. After a time of not seeing him, I wished I had asked his name so I could find out. Even today, years later, I think about him. Did he ever become desperate enough to listen to what he needed to know? If so, was there someone who helped him make his peace with the Lord? Or had I been his last chance—an opportunity that he turned down?

Each one of us comes to Jesus through receiving and believing his promises. My dad's teaching about repentance was very clear. First John 1:8-9 tells us, "If we say we have no sin, we deceive ourselves, and the truth is not in us. If we confess our sins, he is faithful and just, and will forgive our sins and cleanse us from all unrighteousness." We need to confess our sin and be sorry for it, then turn away from our sin and be willing to make a change.

We can then ask Jesus for his salvation. John 3:16 tells us, "For God so loved the world that he gave his only Son, that whoever believes in him should not perish but have eternal life." To receive eternal life we come to Jesus as a little child. We simply ask him for his salvation and believe what he had done for us on the cross. Romans 10:9 explains: "If you confess with your lips that Jesus is Lord and believe in your heart that God raised him from the dead, you will be saved."

When I confessed my sin, said I was sorry for it, and asked forgiveness, I asked Jesus to be my Savior and Lord. I believed in his death for me and also in his resurrection from the dead. Though some people who offer this prayer immediately feel different—full of joy in their new lives—I didn't. Yet there was something I had learned, something I had missed before. We receive salvation through faith, not feelings.

From that moment on, I never again wondered what would happen to me when I died. I *knew*. I would simply pass into the presence of my Lord. I would experience eternal life with him.

My trust in the Lord became even more real as I took the next step—telling others what I believed. That's the promise of Romans 10:10: "For man believes with his heart and so is justified, and he confesses with his lips and so is saved." Or, as the Today's English Version puts it, "It is by our faith that we are put right with God; it is by our confession that we are saved." Each time I told someone what I believed, salvation became more real to me.

Eternal life begins now in the moment we receive the salvation of Jesus Christ. If you would like to be saved from drowning—to be certain that you know where you are going when you die—you have the privilege of being set free in a personal relationship with him. Here are the steps to take:

Confess your sin and ask forgiveness. Pray, "Lord Jesus, I know I have sinned. I confess my sins to you. Yet I believe you died on the cross for my sake. By the power of your blood shed for me, I ask you to forgive me and take away my guilt and sin."

Acknowledge Jesus as your Savior and commit your life to him. Pray, "Lord Jesus, I ask you to be my Savior and Lord over every part of my life. I commit my life totally and completely to you. Thank you that in your death and resurrection you have provided salvation for me. Thank you that in this moment you have set me free, giving me eternal life."

Tell others about your commitment to the Lord. If you prayed the prayers given above or similar words, God has put you right with himself. The promises of Romans 10:9-10 are for you. Through your life and conversation tell others what you believe. Each time you do, it will become more real.

After coming to the Lord in this way, you may say, "I don't feel any different." That's all right. You receive salvation through faith, not feelings. Believe that Jesus Christ has saved you eternally. First John 5:11-13 makes the promise clear:

And this is the testimony, that God gave us eternal life, and this life is in his Son. He who has the Son has life; he who has not the Son of God has not life.

I write this to you who believe in the name of the Son of God, that you may know that you have eternal life. And this is the confidence which we have in him, that if we ask anything according to his will he hears us. And if we know that he hears us in whatever we ask, we know that we have obtained the requests made of him.

Whenever you make a life-changing decision, it's crucial to drive your stake into the ground, to do something that says, "This is what I believe. This is where I stand."

You may wish to fill in these words, or write them in your Bible or at the beginning of this book. It's important to see them in your own handwriting: "On [this day] _____ at [give time] _____ I have confessed my sin and asked for salvation. I have received the assurance that you, Jesus, have given it to me. Thank you, Jesus, that I do not have to be afraid of death. Thank you that you have set me free—free to live because I am free to die. In faith I thank you!"

If doubts arise, return to the verses you have read. Return to the words you have written. Remember that you have committed your life to Christ. Continue to thank him for his salvation and for the eternal life that begins right now, right here, in this moment.

FAITH THOUGHT

BUT GOD SHOWS HIS LOVE FOR US IN THAT WHILE WE WERE YET SINNERS CHRIST DIED FOR US. SINCE, THEREFORE, WE ARE NOW JUSTIFIED [PUT RIGHT] BY HIS BLOOD, MUCH MORE SHALL WE BE SAVED BY HIM FROM THE WRATH OF GOD. . . . FOR THE WAGES OF SIN IS DEATH, BUT THE FREE GIFT OF GOD IS ETERNAL LIFE IN CHRIST JESUS OUR LORD. (ROM. 5:8-9; 6:23)

Thank you, Jesus,
that as I struggle in deep water,
you reach out,
offering the life preserver
of your love and your forgiveness.
Thank you that by dying on the cross
you made salvation a gift
for all who come to you.
I ask your forgiveness for my sins.
I believe that your death
on the cross was for me.
I also ask you to be my Savior
and Lord over every part of my life.
Thank you that eternal life
begins in the moment
I put my trust in you.
Thank you that because I am ready to die
I am free to live!

THE GIFT OF
COMMUNICATION

———◆◆◆———

Who me? Talk with someone?
Tell how I really feel?
You have to be kidding!

I HAD MADE A NUMBER OF VISITS to my cancer specialist when a recently diagnosed patient nodded toward the office door.

"Lois," he asked, "do you ever get used to approaching that door?"

I knew exactly what he meant. Early in my treatments I learned to fool myself. As I entered the medical building, I promised myself something special. *The minute I get out of here, I'm going to . . .* I assured myself that there was something beyond chemotherapy, even if it was just a good breakfast.

On those visits to my oncologist I also prayed for everyone in the office—patients, nurses, technicians, receptionists, and doctors. I knew I was praying to take my mind off chemotherapy, but I didn't think my prayers would be wasted.

Fear often encourages us to play games, even with those we know best. There are times, however, when the games we play aren't helpful. Charlotte, a friend who has also experienced breast cancer, told me how she first dealt with shock, fear, and denial. She'd say to her husband, "When I get over this thing . . ."

Bob would interrupt and ask, "What thing?" He'd make her name it for what it was—breast cancer. His honesty helped her communicate what was really happening to her.

In a similar way my husband and I played a "protect your spouse" game:

Lois: *I won't tell Roy that I'm afraid I'll die. He'll worry about me.*

Roy: *She keeps saying everything is all right. She must be covering up something really awful.*

Though we didn't realize it at first, both of us were telling ourselves, *If I pretend everything is okay, whatever is wrong will go away.* Unfortunately, just the opposite happened. Poor communication multiplies every problem.

Before my surgery, Roy and I thought we talked together. Yet our new circumstances forced us to communicate at a much deeper level. Instead of just asking, "What do you *think* about this?" we learned to also ask, "How do you *feel* about this situation?" As we shared our fears with one another, it lightened the load—on both sides, not just mine or his.

In common with other people facing a life-threatening illness, Roy and I needed to communicate about some crucial issues. *What about my future?* I wondered as a cancer patient. *Will I be able to work? How much pain lies ahead? If it comes to that, will I die with dignity?* I soon realized that it wasn't the dying that made me most afraid. It was the suffering I might experience before death.

My husband's inward questioning took a different form: *What will I do if Lois dies? Where will I bury her? What about our children? What should I do with the house?*

In the first hours after my mastectomy I felt carried in love, surrounded by friends and loved ones. I walked on prayers instead of air. I believed in a big God who could do anything.

As God answered the prayers of countless people, I was able to offer thanksgiving and praise during my hospitalization and in the weeks immediately following. Often I fell asleep praying, "Thank you, Jesus, that you are with me," or, "I praise you, Lord." Not thank you for evil, but thank you for bringing good, even out of cancer.

But then my efforts to communicate took an even more difficult turn. Some well-meaning people told me I wasn't facing reality. They felt I should be more upset, more angry with God. In the time since, I've met enough patients who deny reality that I understand why others were concerned for me. But instead of being angry with God, I became angry with them. I was also deeply hurt. There was something those people didn't know about me, and they never bothered to ask.

A few weeks after my hospitalization a perceptive doctor said to me, "Lois, I don't sense anger in you. Aren't you angry about your mastectomy?"

Later I was angry for other reasons, such as why I had to cope with a diagnosis of cancer while other people were enjoying life. Yet because the doctor asked the right question, I explained what I told few others: "I asked, 'Why, God?' before surgery, while I was still strong. Before this happened, I've needed to ask 'Why?' so many times about other things that I knew I might as well get it over with."

In times of crisis the level of our communication with God will shape what happens in the rest of our lives. In the "Why, God?" moment, some people turn away from God forever. Yet it is at that moment that we most need God's loving arms around us.

I never took it lightly that God used Scripture to tell me that Satan had demanded permission to sift Peter like wheat. I had no doubt that for me, further sifting was ahead. Because of that, I prayed, "Lord, that's the surgery I dread most. Why, God? Why me?" I asked the question honestly, before anyone else knew what I was facing.

In the moment of telling the Lord I trusted him, I came to peace. Afterwards I could not be angry about something I had already relinquished.

Soon Roy and I discovered something else:

> *If we ask him, God will give us*
> *carefully chosen people to come*
> *alongside us in our time of need.*

When our emotional and spiritual needs were very great, a couple came to us and said, "We'd like to be your encouragers during this time." That husband and wife and two other couples from our church met with us at least once a month. Sometimes we simply talked or had fun together. Other times one of us led a Bible study. We ended each evening by praying for one another.

What started as a support group for Roy and me grew into a relationship of mutual support. During the years that we met together, one couple after another needed encouragement in some way. As a result, I never felt that we had just been the takers. In the course of time, we were able to give as well. Even now, years later and separated by many miles, we still feel an instant bond every time we think of those people. The depth of their Christian caring is something we will never forget.

For Roy and me another person carefully chosen by God was a trusted Christian counselor, Vern Bittner. After I was diagnosed with cancer, Roy experienced anticipatory grief. Although it had been twenty years since his first wife died from illness, to Roy it seemed twenty minutes. In addition, he had a difficult work situation and was still grieving from the death of an older brother. Out of a combination of circumstances, Roy went into depression.

Talking about his fears and stresses with someone who had a balanced viewpoint encouraged Roy to pick out essentials and bring them into the light. Vern helped him identify and deal with long-ago hurts, as well as the present crisis. Through counseling Roy learned an important concept: *Depression is anger turned inward.* When he found healthy ways to talk about his anger, Roy communicated feelings he had previously kept inside. Soon he left depression behind. For my part, I needed to be willing to listen to how he felt, even if it involved something I had done wrong.

For anyone who faces a time of testing, it's easy to hesitate in seeking professional help until a problem looms three times its real size. We may give ourselves excuses that keep us from asking for help: "What will other people think? I can handle my own life." Fear and self-pity produce the idea, "I'm the only one suffering this way. No one else will understand." Yet Christian counselors have helped others deal with problems just like ours. Such counselors can help us move more quickly toward healing. In turn we may be able to pass on God's comfort to someone else (2 Cor. 1:3-4).

Each of us can easily identify the replenishers—people in our lives who build us up. My Danish grandmother was that way. In her last years she gave strength and hope to her dying husband. After she joined him in the nursing home, she fell more than once and suffered broken bones. Yet whenever we came to visit, she encouraged us. Often I wondered if she saved up funny stories just for our visits.

One pastor realized I was holding things inside, not asking for needed prayer, and said, "We're your friends. Do us the favor of telling us when you hurt emotionally, so it doesn't build up." Another person wrote, "If you need the space and permission to not be faithfully strong, you have it."

Just as we can seek out those who build us up, so can we recognize the people who weaken or tear us down. My compassionate nature motivates me to be a good listener, but I can pray for another patient without knowing all the details. To my remembrance, however, it was never a patient who gave me a problem, but the person who did not understand what suffering is. I learned to give myself permission to *not* listen to everything that some unwise person wanted to tell me. During an endless story about someone's cancer, I turned my head and began talking with someone else. Or I excused myself from any group that gathered like a pack of dogs tearing meat off a bone.

As time passed and I became physically, emotionally, and spiritually stronger, I had enough positive experiences to know that if we communicate honestly *but wisely* a crisis helps us grow in our most meaningful relationships. As the apostle John writes, "Whoever lives by the truth comes into the light, so that it may be seen plainly that what he has done has been done through God" (John 3:21, NIV).

It reassures me that the same Peter made bold by the Spirit at Pentecost once was as afraid as I sometimes am. When he saw Jesus, Peter leaped from the boat and walked on the storm-tossed Sea of Galilee. From a human point of view that took a great deal of faith. But then Peter saw the strong wind, became afraid, and began to sink. "Lord, save me!" he cried. Reaching out his hand, Jesus caught Peter and said, "O man of little faith, why did you doubt?" (Matt. 14:31).

If my fears and doubts are to be conquered, I cannot look at the wind or the waves, nor to myself. I must keep my eyes on Christ, walking on the water of healthy communication with him and with others. In doing so, I allow the Lord to send the right person to me—someone who offers encouragement, even without knowing how desperately I need it.

Soon after being diagnosed with cancer, I attended my Danish grandmother's funeral. As I drove the many miles to her home congregation, I wondered, *How am I going to feel sitting in church? Will the next gathering of the relatives be for me?* Entering the church, I prayed, "Lord, give me your protection from fear."

Two hours later, I stood at Grandma's graveside. When the committal service was over, I thanked the pastor for his message of the resurrection. He recognized me and looked straight into my eyes. As he spoke, I knew God had been at work, both in him and in me.

"Lois," the pastor said, "you may come to many funerals before others come to yours."

Faith Thought

FEAR NOT, FOR I AM WITH YOU, BE NOT DISMAYED, FOR I AM YOUR GOD; I WILL STRENGTHEN YOU, I WILL HELP YOU, I WILL UPHOLD YOU WITH MY VICTORIOUS RIGHT HAND. (ISA. 41:10)

Jesus,
help my loved ones and me
not to separate ourselves
from one another,
forming islands
in our way of thinking
and our way of doing things.
Instead, make us willing to
continue learning
about and from one another.
Help us communicate
with honesty and caring,
support and encouragement.
Make us peninsulas, Jesus,
joined to you, connected,
yet reaching out to others
in the ocean of your love.

CHAPTER SIX

ALL THINGS, LORD?

———◆●◆———

I don't like to say it, God,
but I can't help thinking that
you could have given me a better deal.
Why am I the one who has to suffer?
Why me, God?

MANY YEARS BEFORE I WAS DIAGNOSED WITH CANCER, a school nurse stopped to see me. Her timing was not the best. Problems had piled up, and I was anxious about a serious long-term illness of one of our children. I remember trying to be pleasant, but my real feelings must have shown through.

Without warning, the nurse changed the subject. "Lois," she said gently, "the Lord chastens the people he loves."

Only my mother's awesome attempts to instill good manners kept me from throwing a book. I almost stormed out of the room, crying, "Then, Lord, don't love me so much!" Instead tears welled into my eyes. I was unable to speak.

In that moment the nurse added a second verse: "All things work together for those who love the Lord." *It's a cliche,* I thought, though I knew Romans 8:28. *I don't believe it!*

Several months later the nurse died, and I discovered something. At the time she visited me, she was struggling with cancer. The words she spoke had no doubt been a comfort to her. Yet because that kind of comfort bothered me, I kept thinking about the verses she quoted.

Since then I've learned that few, if any, people are able to go through life without facing a "Why, God?" situation. We hear bad news and tell ourselves, *It can't be true. Maybe I'll wake up, and find it's just a nightmare.* But even as we try to deny the truth, someone repeats the bad news. We fight against belief. *Maybe if I don't talk about it . . . Maybe if I don't believe what I'm hearing, it won't be true.*

The initial numbness, our state of disbelief, is perhaps the Lord's kindness. As a wise pastor once told me, "I believe the numbness of grief is God's protection until we reach the place where we can handle more."

Whatever the cause, the reality of grief brings a struggle. No longer separated by race, sex, economic status, or creed, those who suffer become one. Whatever our walk in life, grief acts as a common denominator, bringing all of us who question to a level of desperate need.

As I look back, my conversation with the nurse was the beginning of a series of times when I asked deeply felt questions. Many of those moments were connected with the illness or death of loved ones; others were not. Yet with every form of suffering, I joined all humanity in needing to pass through the stages of grief identified by Dr. Elisabeth Kübler-Ross in her book *On Death and Dying.* Christians sometimes hope they can bypass those stages, but it doesn't work that way.

Each of us takes these stages of denial, anger, bargaining, depression, and acceptance as an individual. We have different growth times and different levels of experience for dealing with suffering. Sometimes we mix the order of our grieving a bit, or return to a certain emotion before going on again. Often the rate at which we pass through the stages of grief depends on how close we are to the trouble spot or the depth of our relationship with the person involved. Before long, the numbness of shock changes to a searing pain out of which we ask, "Why, God? Why me?" or, "Why my loved one?"

In the moment of asking, "Why, God?" we stand with Mary Magdalene outside the Lord's tomb. When the angels asked her, "Woman, why are you weeping?" she answered, "Because they have taken away my Lord, and I do not know where they have laid him" (John 20:13). Whether we as patients receive bad news or we have a loved one who suffers, we ask the same question: "Is everything lost, even my faith? Is all that I believed in, hoped for, and dreamed about gone forever?"

When facing different forms of crisis, I have known the emptiness when for a time even Scripture did not seem real, for I lost the belief that the promises were for me. The knife is thrust deep, turns, and widens the wound. While that wound is fresh, I feel I cannot pray. I seem unable to stop the flow of blood. Aching in every bone, I can only utter the name, "Lord God, Lord God, Lord God . . ."

Before my mastectomy, I had faced other "Why, God?" times. One of the crucial ones started with a telephone call on a crisp October day ablaze with the full color of autumn. I learned that the cancer of Roy's fifty-three-year-old brother, Harvey, had spread even more than we feared. After hanging up the phone, I went outside and sat down. I looked across the backyard to red oak leaves, sun-dappled to orange. Above them shone a brilliant sky.

I wondered how the world could be that beautiful in the midst of such terrible suffering. I knew that for Harv anesthetic and hospital walls blocked the view of autumn splendor. Then came the inevitable question: "Why Harv, God? His wife and three children are still young."

In the blackness of the night that followed, other thoughts came. I woke up aching, suddenly remembering, and wishing the oblivion of sleep. Before I knew it, I spoke aloud: "God, I'm angry. I hate you." As my sleeping husband rolled over, I silenced my voice, but my thoughts continued. *Why did you allow this to happen to my husband's family? You could have stopped it. Already they've lost too many, too young.*

Contrary to what some people may expect, I was not struck dead for my anger with God. What might seem blasphemy was simply the agonized cry of my inner spirit. I suspect God recognized it as such.

It was not until years later when I faced cancer myself that I began to understand the real significance of that prayer. If I give the Lord and his people the opportunity to help, it's possible to pass through the stages of grief more quickly. What are some ideas that can encourage us in our times of questioning?

Being Honest with God

One day I talked with a nurse who had worked with many cancer patients. "I find that for a time many religious patients who face life-threatening illness are handicapped by their beliefs," she said. "They're afraid to express their anger, to say, 'Why, God?' They think they are losing their faith, or feel guilty because they question God's omnipotence."

Usually I ask, "Why, God?" out of sorrow or anger over something that has happened. But often my feeling about the past or present mixes with my apprehension over the future. C. S. Lewis described it well after the death of his wife, Joy, when he wrote, "No one ever told me that grief felt so like fear" *(Grief Observed)*.

Fear mounts as I combine emotionally the yesterdays, todays, and tomorrows in one awesome threat. Other times I ask, "Why?" out of a feeling I don't recognize at first. Then I understand what it is. I have been "good." Therefore shouldn't I be rewarded? Shouldn't I experience blessing, not pain, in my life?

Jeremiah knew the feeling: "Why does the way of the wicked prosper? Why do all the faithless live at ease? You have planted them, and they have taken root; they grow and bear fruit" (Jer. 12:1-2 NIV). In Psalm 30, David put it another way: "What profit is there in my death, if I go down to the Pit? Will the dust praise thee? Will it tell of thy faithfulness? Hear, O Lord, and be gracious to me! O Lord, be thou my helper!" (vv. 9-10).

Prayer gives us the opportunity to express anger. "Why?" is a question every one of us must ask when we come to that point of loss where life no longer makes sense. If we don't express our anger to God or someone else during a crisis, we will need to do so later—perhaps years later. It's healthier to ask, "Why?" right away.

It's important to be honest, not only with God, but also with those around us. The anger of grief comes out in all kinds of unexpected ways. In our grieving, we often flail out. Sometimes others get in our path. If they don't understand what's wrong, our anger frightens them away.

When angry, we are even more vulnerable to hurt. The deeper our suffering, the greater the potential for loneliness. At times we put ourselves in a lonely place because we don't want to bother other people with our troubles. We think they're too busy or won't understand. In our desire to be strong we shut them out. Or we want to hide what might, after all, be somehow our fault.

On the other hand, none of those things may be true. Our anger may increase because we feel ignored in our suffering. We don't sense the support of others. They don't seem to care. For one man who had consistently helped countless people, a lack of support in his time of need was the deepest hurt of all: "How can people *not* notice when my hurt is so big? How can my pain be this terrible and the people I've spent hours helping not take a moment to offer comfort?"

Why, God? Why?

Hearing the Truth

For many years I misunderstood the goodness of God because of my anger about the conversation with the school nurse. Often I felt guilty. More than once, I pushed aside the thought that God was getting even or, worse still, loving me too much. I wanted to believe in a good God. Yet each time I faced another difficulty, I came to Christ with a question. "Did I sin? Have I done something wrong?"

When his disciples saw a man blind from birth, they asked Jesus, "Who sinned, this man or his parents, that he was born blind?" Jesus answered, "It was not that this man sinned, or his parents, but that the works of God might be made manifest in him" (John 9:2-3).

My own father, a retired pastor, explained the difference between the chastisement mentioned by the nurse (Heb. 12:5-9; Prov. 3:11-12) and the suffering of illness: "God doesn't teach, 'An eye for an eye, a tooth for a tooth.' The end of chastisement in Scripture is not to beat us down. Rather, it's to lead us out into a fuller, richer life. Take, for example, the prodigal son. When he lost all his money, his poverty wasn't an end in itself. Instead it was the means which brought him to a new realization—'I want to return to my father.' In the same way, when we suffer, God in love reaches out to give us new experiences in grace."

Another pastor told me, "Lois, the corrections of the Lord are not the premature deaths of loved ones. His corrections come in a way that we almost smile at ourselves."

Even so, through the years a question remained at the back of my mind. All things work together for those who love the Lord? All things, Lord? *All* things?

Only after I woke up from having a mastectomy did I fully believe Romans 8:28. For the first time I felt the impact of the verse as it is translated in the Revised Standard Version: "We know that in everything God works for good with those who love him, who are called according to his purpose."

In everything? God works *in everything* to bring good? As a Christian, I'm called according to his purpose. In being called, I discovered there are circumstances more difficult to face than a mastectomy. But even when I don't understand how God works, the promise is that *in everything he works for good.* While still groggy from anesthetic, I saw God bringing good, even out of cancer. Situations about which I had prayed for months began changing around my bedside.

Many people continued to pray daily for me, and those prayers carried me through the time when I had to learn the discipline of praise. If unable to say words of praise, I sang old hymns or new spiritual songs. Out of that obedience I lived the meaning of Nehemiah 8:10: "The joy of the Lord is your strength."

Through prayer and that offering of praise, the Lord deepened my understanding of who he is. God does not cause the various forms of cancer I've faced. It's true, he allowed physical cancer to come to me. But while he allows something with one hand, he stands ready, holding in his other hand the resources he wants to give me to help. If my anger keeps me from turning to him, I push away his comfort. I refuse his gifts of strength, peace, and joy.

When I'm honest, I can pray, "I'm angry that this has come to me, but I believe you did not cause it." I can also say, "Lord, you have not allowed this to happen without at the same time promising the strength I need. And so, Lord, I release the whole situation to you, knowing that you will act in the best way possible."

In *My Utmost for His Highest* Oswald Chambers puts it this way: "Never confuse the trial of faith with the ordinary discipline of life, because a great deal of what we call the trial of faith is the inevitable result of being alive."

Whether we experience a trial that is an ordinary part of being alive or something that is meant to help us grow in positive ways, we make a choice. How are we going to respond to God? In whatever comes to us, there's a life principle:

We can let our "Why, God?"
questions drive us away from
him, or we can throw ourselves and
our questions into his loving arms.

Discovering the Life

If we turn to him in spite of our suffering, we hear a cry from the darkness. From the cross comes Christ's lament: "My God, my God, why hast thou forsaken me?" (Mark 15:34).

"Why, God? Why have you forsaken me?" And we begin to understand that Jesus knew a separation greater than any we will ever know. To bear the sin of the world—our sin—as true God and true man, Jesus had to be apart from the Father he loved so

much. Apart from the holy God who created the plan by which
we are saved. That same holy God reaches out, wanting to lead us
into new life.

Yet before healing comes, there's another step. Author and
editor Joseph Bayly lost three children through death, and his
book *Psalms of My Life* includes many poems originally not written for publication. In "A Psalm on the Death of an 18-year-old
Son," he utters a poignant "Why, God?":

> *What waste Lord*
> *this ointment precious*
> *here outpoured*
> *is treasure great*
> *beyond my mind to think.*
> *For years*
> *until this midnight*
> *it was safe*
> *contained*
> *awaiting careful use*
> *now broken*
> *wasted*
> *lost.*
> *The world is poor*
> *so poor it needs each drop*
> *of such a store.*
> *This treasure spent*
> *might feed a multitude*
> *for all their days*
> *and then yield more.*
> *This world is poor?*
> *It's poorer now*
> *the treasure's lost.*
> *I breathe its lingering fragrance*
> *soon even that*
> *will cease.*
> *What purpose served?*

The act is void of reason
sense
Lord
madmen do such deeds
not sane.
The sane man hoards his treasure
spends with care
if good
to feed the poor
or else to feed himself.
Let me alone Lord
you've taken from me
what I'd give Your world.
I cannot see such waste
that You should take
what poor men need.
You have a heaven
full of treasure
could You not wait
to exercise Your claim
on this?
O spare me Lord forgive
that I may see
beyond this world
beyond myself
Your sovereign plan
or seeing not
may trust You
Spoiler of my treasure.
Have mercy Lord
here is my quitclaim.

"My quitclaim." In the power of his relinquishment, Joe's words speak to us. "Here is the transfer of my right," he says. "My right to my irreplaceable eighteen-year-old son. The son I loved and cared for all of his life."

When at last we can do no more, we come to that point of relinquishment—of giving over all that we hold most dear. And with relinquishment there comes at last a measure of peace. "Here, Lord, is my son," Joe said in his memorable way. "Though I do not see or understand, I choose to trust you, Lord. I choose to give my son to you."

No longer are the circumstances of life most important. What matters is whether we sense Christ's presence in the midst of them. In every dark place where we allow him to enter, he brings the light of his presence. Knowing his presence counts above all else.

"I love Harv's wife, Betty," God assured me in those days of grieving. "I love each of his children—Cheri, Karin, and John Harvey. Even in death I will be victorious."

Harv's funeral was held in the church he pastored—a large white frame church with a tall steeple. I will never forget the sound of singing that day. Nor will I forget the partly built church behind the one where we worshiped.

Harvey had led his congregation in planning that church and guiding its construction. When he became too sick to walk through the building, he watched it go up from the window of his home. The day of his funeral, workers placed the large steel girders for the roof.

It's not finished I thought, and again felt angry. *Harvey didn't get to see it finished.*

But when the funeral was over and the new church was almost completed, Betty used the memorial money to buy the large cross that would hang at the front of the sanctuary.

Before the cross was raised into position, Betty, Cheri, Karin, and John Harvey went over to the church. They took a black marker and wrote on the wood at the top of the cross where it couldn't be seen from below. They wrote God's promise of Romans 8:39: "Nothing will be able to separate us from the love of God that is in Christ Jesus our Lord." Then they added their names: Betty, Cheri, Karin, John.

Nothing, not even the questions of "Why, God?" and the things we don't understand, can separate us from the love of God.

He Shares Our Pain

On the way home from a trip, Roy and I stopped to visit my cousin Naomi and her husband, Tom Gutt. Not wanting to miss their Wednesday evening Bible study, they brought us to their church, First United Methodist, in downtown Oklahoma City. In their enthusiasm for all that was happening there, they gave us a tour of the building.

As we stood in a doorway, looking across to the Alfred P. Murrah Federal Building, Tom told us about the Loaves and Fishes program held for people who work in the downtown business community. "Many of them work in the federal building just across the street," Tom said. "On Thursday noon they come and eat lunch while Pastor Nick leads them in Bible study. Each week more and more people come."

But exactly one week later the terrorist bomb exploded, and 168 people died. The realization of our vulnerability changed our perspective as Americans forever.

In the midst of local and national grieving, as well as their need to deal with the destruction in their own buildings, the members of First Methodist wanted to reach out to others. They felt led to construct a small outdoor chapel where those who grieved could stop, rest, and pray. Although the chapel included a large cross, members of the Jewish Federation of Greater Oklahoma City and an Islamic community contributed to the construction. "There is in Jewish life a phrase 'tikun alom,'" said Edie Roodman, executive director of the Jewish Federation, in an article by Pat Gilliland in the *Daily Oklahoman*. "It means 'repair of the world.' I think our fund reflects a deep commitment to that."

During the years since the 1995 bombing, thousands of people have stopped in that small chapel with the view of where the federal building once stood. In the national memorial on the Murrah Building site, 168 empty chairs are placed in the location where each person sat when he or she died. Beyond that memorial and across another street is a statue constructed by St.

Joseph's Catholic Church. The statue's powerful image represents a tall, white-robed Christ. He stands with his back to the busy street and the place where the federal building once stood. The representation of Christ faces a brick wall in which there are 168 empty spaces—one space for each person who died. With bowed head Jesus faces that symbol of loss, covers his face with one hand, and weeps.

In whatever suffering we know, in whatever "Why, God?" we ask, we cannot forget one important truth: Jesus Christ weeps with us.

To all who suffer, standing with Mary outside the empty tomb, the angel says, "Fear not." Though at times we cannot see Christ, nor hear his words of comfort, the reason for our faith is nevertheless alive.

"Fear not," the angel says. "You have not lost everything, though it seems so. All that he told you was true. He is risen."

He is risen indeed.

———————◆—————————

FAITH THOUGHT

WHEN JESUS SAW HER WEEPING, AND THE JEWS WHO CAME WITH HER ALSO WEEPING, HE WAS DEEPLY MOVED IN SPIRIT AND TROUBLED; AND HE SAID, "WHERE HAVE YOU LAID HIM?" THEY SAID TO HIM, "LORD, COME AND SEE." JESUS WEPT. (JOHN 11:33-35)

Must I, like Thomas,
go out into the night
to stumble on a dusty street,
heartsick, afraid, my darkness
more than sun gone down?
Each time I wonder if he walked alone

I stagger through my questions, doubts,
until at last returning
to the locked but friend-filled room.
Still, Lord, you understood
the needs of Thomas,
and to me you say,
"See my nail prints? Touch my side."
Those costly words
and possible reopening of your wounds
teach me yet more of your compassion,
your willingness to offer gifts
of trust and faith.
My Lord, my God,
make me one of those
who, without sight, believe.

PRAYER THAT MAKES A DIFFERENCE

———————◆◆———————

I need to pray
as I've never prayed before.
How can I ask the Lord
for really difficult things?

O NE OF HIS DISCIPLES saw Jesus praying and asked, "Lord, teach us to pray, just as John taught his disciples." The request sprang from a childlike faith, and Jesus spoke just as directly. His words cover every aspect of our daily need:

When you pray, say this:
"Father:
May your holy name be honored;
may your Kingdom come.
Give us day by day the food we need.
Forgive us our sins,
for we forgive everyone who does us wrong.
And do not bring us to hard testing." (Luke 11:1-4 TEV)

Too often I forget the simplicity and yet the depth of that prayer. Nowhere does Christ say, "I want to make prayer so hard that only a few people can talk to my Father." Instead Jesus told his disciples, "Whoever does not receive the kingdom of God like a child shall not enter it" (Luke 18:17). Not only do we enter the kingdom, but we learn the conversation of prayer as a child. There's another life principle involved:

> *Through the relationship of prayer,*
> *we learn to ask in childlike faith*
> *yet with the authority given by Jesus.*

What are some key ideas to help us increase our effectiveness in prayer?

Relationship

Every one of us needs to be valued as a person. To be regarded as an individual, not a number, nor a commodity. We each like to be considered a worthy person, not because of what we have accomplished or the money we've earned but because of who we are.

God gives that very reason for loving us. He loves us the way we are. In fact, he created us that way. More than that, we belong to him. Even as we want to know the human beings that we love, we have the privilege of growing in the way we know Jesus.

"Prayer is the language of a relationship," Hallesby tells us. Prayer is the way we communicate. Our Lord pays such close attention to those things about which we pray that we enter into the closest possible relationship.

Jesus compares this relationship to a grapevine and its branches: "I am the vine, you are the branches. He who abides in me, and I in him, he it is that bears much fruit, for apart from me you can do nothing" (John 15:5). To the person who remains in Christ comes one of the great prayer promises: "If you abide in me, and my words abide in you, ask whatever you will, and it shall be done for you" (John 15:7).

This promise does not mean that we can recklessly ask for any foolish wish that comes to us. The promise is dependent on our keeping of the condition, "If you abide in me." If we remain in Christ, living deeply in him, we ask out of our shared relationship. We know him so well that we ask for those things he delights to give.

In my months on chemotherapy, I sometimes felt alone as I prayed, as though whatever happened were dependent on me. In a sense that can be true, for there may not be anyone else who cares enough to offer a needed prayer. Yet in another sense that thought is never true. As I rediscovered life as the gift that it is, my relationship in prayer brought me to a new awareness of all that it means to belong to the Lord.

As a young mother I sometimes needed help from my neighbor. Our good relationship gave me the right to ask. If I balance my requests with praise, thanksgiving, and confession, my healthy relationship with God gives me the same right. In *The Wonder of Being Loved* Alvin Rogness puts it well by praying, "Lord, help me to keep bothering you."

A Cleansed Spirit

We need to see sin as God sees it— an offense to his holiness. The psalmist makes it very clear: "If I had cherished iniquity in my heart, the Lord would not have listened" (Ps. 66:18).

Iniquity, or sin, is anything that separates us from God. God gives us a cleansed spirit when we are sorry for our sin and ask to be forgiven. When asking forgiveness, it's helpful to specifically name the sin before God. Sometimes that sin includes something I did. At other times there is something I should have done but didn't. I also ask the Lord to cleanse my conscious and subconscious thoughts.

In other words, I'm praying, "I'm sorry for the ways I hurt others. I'm sorry for the ways I've hurt you, Lord. I ask for your forgiveness, your cleansing. I want to be clean before you."

David fell into sin with Bathsheba and made things even worse by planning the murder of her husband. But when David came under conviction, a cry rose from the depths of his heart. In

Psalm 51:1-2 he pleads, "Have mercy on me, O God, according to thy steadfast love; according to thy abundant mercy blot out my transgressions. Wash me thoroughly from my iniquity, and cleanse me from my sin!"

David took sin seriously, and so should we. If we wish to receive answered prayer, we should first echo David's plea, "Create in me a clean heart, O God, and put a new and right spirit within me. Cast me not away from thy presence, and take not thy holy Spirit from me" (Ps. 51:10-11).

A Thankful, Praise-Filled Attitude

In Philippians 4:4-6 Paul tells us, "Rejoice in the Lord always; again I will say, Rejoice! Let all men know your forbearance. The Lord is at hand. Have no anxiety about anything, but in everything by prayer and supplication with thanksgiving let your requests be made known to God." Paul does not tell us to be thankful *for* everything, including evil. Instead he urges us to ask with a thankful spirit, no matter what is happening to us.

In his Times Square Church pulpit series, David Wilkerson explains the difference. There is a certain kind of praying that displeases God because our requests come out of a despondent, defeatist attitude.

David calls it "sniveling." A sniveling in which we forget the faithfulness of the Lord. All that he has done *for* us in the past. All that he has done *in* us. And all that he has done *through* us. David asks, "How must the Lord feel when we beg him to meet and supply all of our future needs, and yet we discredit what he has already done for us in the past?"

Since I'm quite good at sniveling, David's words struck home. In the months immediately after surgery, I had no choice but to begin praising God and thanking him with my will. Often I did so with tears running down my cheeks. But as life became easier, I forgot the secret of a thankful heart. When circumstances again became extremely difficult, I needed to relearn that position in prayer. It's important to thank God, even in the moment we ask, long before we see the answer.

If we value our time with the Lord, we experience his nearness. We commit ourselves to pray, "Lord Jesus Christ, I thank and praise you for who you are. You have delivered me from my sins. It's no problem for you to take care of all my spiritual, physical, intellectual, and emotional needs. In your name I lay before you those specific needs. In faith I thank you in advance for all that you are going to do."

Heartfelt, Specific Desires

Blind Bartimaeus called out, "Jesus, Son of David, have mercy on me!" When people told him to be quiet he shouted again, "Son of David, have mercy on me!"

Bartimaeus expected something to happen. No doubt Jesus knew what he needed, but he encouraged him to ask specifically: "What do you want me to do for you?"

The blind man replied, "Master, let me receive my sight."

"Go your way," Jesus answered, "your faith has made you well" (Mark 10:46-52).

When we use the small amount of faith we have, the Lord gives us more. The first book of Samuel tells about an ordinary woman named Hannah who suffered under the treatment of her husband's other wife. Hannah's honest need to present her husband with an heir became a deep desire.

Australian Bible teacher Ken Chant talked about the motivation of a deep desire. He referred to Psalm 81:10-16 NIV, where God reminds his people of his caring nature: "I am the Lord your God, who brought you up out of Egypt. Open wide your mouth and I will fill it." Then we sense the grieving in his voice: "But my people would not listen to me; Israel would not submit to me. So I gave them over to their stubborn hearts to follow their own devices."

God wanted to give abundance, but his idolatrous people refused it. After a long insistence on their own way, God finally gave them what they actually wanted. The nation reaped the misery of its own choice.

Chant explained: "God will give you what you really want—whether heaven or hell, righteousness or sin."

For a long time I prayed for someone's salvation before I sensed the gentle correction of the Holy Spirit: "What is it you really want, Lois? Your motives are mixed. Do you want that person to become a Christian because of the way she treats you? Or because she needs to know Jesus? Be honest before God about how you really feel."

Out of Hannah's deep desire came Samuel's birth (1 Sam. 1:10-11). But Hannah made painful choices. When Samuel was still very young, she took him to the temple and gave him over to the Lord. In time Samuel was recognized as a prophet, priest, and intercessor of amazing spiritual and historical significance in the sight of God and others. When disintegration threatened Israel, he pulled the nation together, becoming its second founder.

Authority in His Name

A Roman centurion came to Jesus, asking for help: "Lord," he said, "my servant lies at home paralyzed and in terrible suffering."

Jesus said to him, "I will go and heal him."

The centurion replied, "Lord, I do not deserve to have you come under my roof. But just say the word, and my servant will be healed. For I myself am a man under authority, with soldiers under me. I tell this one, 'Go,' and he goes; and that one, 'Come,' and he comes. I say to my servant, 'Do this,' and he does it."

Jesus was astonished and said to those following him, "I tell you the truth, I have not found anyone in Israel with such great faith." To the centurion, Jesus said, "Go! It will be done for you just as you believed it would." The centurion's servant was healed that very hour (Matt. 8:5-13 NIV).

What does it mean to pray with authority? In whatever prayer we offer, the power comes in looking to Jesus and praying in his name. He gives us authority if we use his name in the right way—reverently and in a way that is consistent with the nature of Jesus.

Often I ask that the Holy Spirit give me scriptural principles and examples in the area for which I pray. In his role as helper and counselor, the Holy Spirit shows us all that Jesus can do. Read Acts 3 and Acts 4:1-22 for an incredible example of the power of praying in the name of Jesus.

At first our steps in praying may be hesitant, even as Peter's upon the water. Yet each time we immerse ourselves in Scripture, then depend wholeheartedly on the Lord, we not only grow in knowing him but also in the boldness of prayer. We realize, like the centurion, that Jesus is a man of authority.

Jesus never claimed to have that authority in his own right. It was given to him (Matt. 28:18-19). Even as the Father gave authority to Jesus, so Jesus gave authority to his disciples. Calling the Twelve together, he "gave them power and authority over all demons and to cure diseases, and he sent them out to preach the kingdom of God and to heal" (Luke 9:1-2).

Out of that same authority, Jesus appointed seventy others and sent them out two by two. When they returned, filled with joy about all that had happened, he replied, "I saw Satan fall like lightning from heaven. Behold, I have given you authority to tread upon serpents and scorpions, and over all the power of the enemy; and nothing shall hurt you" (Luke 10:18-19).

Authority is given in the moment we need it, for the people and situations about which God wants us to pray. Often he expects us to pray about the needs he places right in front of us.

Authority is given through the blood of Jesus and the power of his name. For three years I suffered from a deep emotional wound. I went through the stages of grief, forgave the person involved, asked forgiveness, received counseling from two pastors, and thought I had taken care of everything. Even so, whenever I remembered the circumstances, I felt pain as though a knife turned within.

At God's chosen time, he brought a third pastor into my life. As he prayed, he said, "Don't think of me. Don't think of the circumstances. Think of the name of Jesus."

In that moment I saw the word *Jesus* in bold, black letters. Within the outline of the letters twinkled countless small lights. Behind the word another light glowed, as I spoke the name of Jesus.

Even now, I remember all the circumstances of the incident from which I suffered. Yet whenever I think about the situation, I feel no pain. Only the peace of Jesus.

Commitment to What God Wants

As we pray in the name of Jesus, we ask in faith and hope to see a *yes*. But what if that's not what we receive? Often we think that only *Yes!* is an answer, but God may give us a *No*, or a *Wait*, or a *Get up and get going!* More than once I've had to give over to God my desire for how a prayer is answered. As I reluctantly did so, I discovered that his answers are much better than anything I could possibly imagine.

When we know God's will about an area for which we pray, we are able to ask in greater faith. Without doubt it is his will that all people be saved. We also have the certainty that he wants everyone to live in the power of his Spirit. The truths of Scripture guide us in knowing how to pray.

It's also important to be committed to what *God* wants to do. Job revealed an amazing growth in faith when he said, "Though he slay me, yet will I trust in him" (Job 13:15 KJV). When we seek the Lord, it's our responsibility to pray, his to answer.

If we commit ourselves to God's best purpose, our attitude becomes a vital fiber in the fabric of our prayer life. We say with Paul, "I count everything as loss because of the surpassing worth of knowing Christ Jesus my Lord" (Phil. 3:8). Or with the psalmist, "But for me it is good to be near God; I have made the Lord God my refuge, that I may tell of all thy works" (Ps. 73:28).

As a cancer patient, I found myself especially vulnerable to the cancer of envy. Soon after my mastectomy, I prayed with a friend who had found a lump the size of a walnut. After the breast biopsy, the surgeon said, "When I saw the tumor I was sure it would be cancer. But when I cut it open, it wasn't."

Even as I said, "Thank you, Jesus," the thought came, *She didn't have to have a mastectomy, but I did.* I had to deal with that dark thought immediately, for I knew it would destroy my commitment to pray for others. I began to pray, "Thank you, Jesus, that she *didn't* need a mastectomy." Within a few hours, he filled me with peace and joy, enabling me to be happy for the other woman.

In giving me spiritual, emotional, and physical light, the Lord defends me against every form of darkness. His cross and empty tomb give the promise of ultimate protection. Whatever happens to me, I look ahead, knowing I have eternal life.

Readiness for Battle

If, as Hallesby says in his book *Prayer,* only those who are helpless can truly pray, why do we need to be equipped for battle? When you and I discover the simplicity and the joy of prayer within a loving relationship, we lay hold of a power that threatens Satan. Satan recognizes that power as one through which kingdoms can be changed. He knows that as we grow in our prayer life, we dare to ask difficult things from the Father who is also the ruler of the universe. Satan doesn't want that to happen.

Battles in prayer can be waged even by those who are bedridden, but not by those who are spiritually weak. To prepare for battle we need to pray daily and by name for protection of ourselves and our loved ones. We also need to guard against the forms of darkness that could keep us from seeing the light of Christ.

No soldier who values his life enters a war zone without knowing where the battle is waged. A Christian's battle takes place in the spiritual realm, for Paul warns, "We are not contending against flesh and blood, but against the principalities, against the powers, against the world rulers of this present darkness, against the spiritual hosts of wickedness in the heavenly places."

Paul also tells us what to do about the situation: "Therefore take the whole armor of God, that you may be able to withstand in the evil day, and having done all, to stand" (Eph. 6:12-13).

If we wish to stand firm in prayer, we need to pray on that armor. Each piece covers a specific area of vulnerability—intellectual, emotional, physical, or spiritual (Eph. 6:14-18). We also need to remember the difference between human and divine stubbornness. The first insists on what we want. The second is a God-given perseverance that places us in the front lines of a battle from which we dare not retreat.

Faith beyond Feelings

A sense of the Father's love is an important preparation for effective prayer. Through that love, he shows us how to ask and makes us aware of the prayers he delights in answering. The deeper our understanding of his care for us, the more eager we are to pray.

We experience prayer power in direct proportion to the degree in which we rely on the Lord. "I believe there's a God," a young man told me. "There has to be something behind all this." His outstretched arm indicated the universe. "But I'm not sure Jesus is more than a historical figure. How do I know he's living? When I try to pray, I don't feel anything."

When Christ does not seem real to us, it may be because we don't truly believe in him. Or we're explaining away his answers to prayer. Or we're hiding sin in our heart. It may be time to ask, "Jesus, please make yourself real to me."

If we lack peace about something, it's important to pay attention to that feeling and deal with its cause. But in other situations most of us place too much importance on how we feel. My eighteen months on chemotherapy taught me something. As the dosage increased, the joy and sense of aliveness I normally experience diminished, leaving me feeling dead inside. During that time I pinned a sentence to the curtain above my kitchen sink, because I needed to see it often: "The Christian life is a walk of faith, not of feelings."

If we move ahead, trusting Jesus like a child, he will fill in the needed emotions. A fervent feeling about something makes it easier to pray, but feelings do not determine whether Jesus listens. At times it's necessary to pray with the mind because emotions interfere.

Big or Small Requests

When I lost most of my hair through chemotherapy, I did so gradually over a period of two months. In many ways that was more difficult than my mastectomy. Each time I rolled over at night I collected a mouthful of hair from my pillow. When I prepared a meal, I wondered if I would serve a plateful of hair. Losing one strand at a time is a small thing, but losing a head full of hair looms large. So who is a fair judge of whether God should be bothered?

In Luke's gospel Jesus tells us that even the hairs of our head are numbered (Luke 12:7). Occasionally, I asked, "Lord, are you managing to keep count?" But it helped me to remember that if he cares about details as small as hair, he also cares about my family and all that happens to me.

While deeply discouraged about my appearance, I sensed God's encouragement—words that comforted me throughout the months my hair was sparse: "Lois, I have seen your hairs as they fall to your shoulders, as they drift to the ground. They will be my glory and they shall once again be your glory."

In time my hair did grow back and was a nicer quality than it had been in years. Still as fine as baby's hair, it has a natural wave in humid weather and is a special part of who I am. When someone says, "Lois, your hair is lovely," I smile and say, "Thank you." If there's time, I tell them about God's promise: *Your hair will be my glory, and once again will be your glory.*

The Nudge to Reach Out

During my eighteen months on chemotherapy, I became so involved in praying for others that I often forgot my doctors' diagnosis of cancer. I was not neglecting my health. Yet one day a squirming thought entered my head: *Maybe you should spend whatever power God gives you on praying for yourself.*

Aha! Sounds a bit selfish, doesn't it? But that's the way I am. Immediately I remembered Christ's words, "If any man would come after me, let him deny himself and take up his cross and follow me. For whoever would save his life will lose it; and whoever loses his life for my sake and the gospel's will save it" (Mark 8:34-35).

When I thought about the situation, I realized how much it meant to me to intercede for others, even if I had to pray when too weak to do anything else. Out of the inspiration of that moment I prayed, "Lord, if I am to die of cancer, I ask you to keep my mind alert to the end so I can pray for loved ones."

If we allow him, Jesus goes ahead of us. He knows our needs and separates them from wants that would hinder our growth. He also calls attention to the needs of others.

What does it mean to pray, or intercede, on behalf of others? My dictionary defines the word *intercede* as "to plead on another's behalf." Sometimes the people for whom I plead are individuals I care deeply about. Other times I do not even know the people involved, but feel concerned about them. I believe that nudging, or prompting to pray for them, comes from the Lord.

From another intercessor I learned what it means to call people part of her "bundle." With certain people I make a commitment to pray for them regularly, usually on a daily basis. Members of my family automatically belong to this group. Frequently I meet others about whom the Spirit prompts me to pray, "Lord, make that person part of my bundle. Remind me when that individual needs prayer."

The consistency with which the Holy Spirit honors such a prayer encourages my faith. In common with numerous Christians, I experience a reminding versus a forgetting. This forgetting is not an absence of caring. I sense, rather, that someone is not my prayer responsibility or something is not my burden. If, on the other hand, the Spirit prompts me to pray for someone, I have learned I should not ignore that nudge. Usually the Holy Spirit leads me to pray at just the time when that person needs it. The Lord's gift to me becomes my gift to others.

In the more than twenty-three years since I wrote the earlier edition of this book, methods of diagnosis and treatment options for people with breast cancer have greatly improved. I was still on chemo and faced all the uncertainties of a recent diagnosis of cancer. Yet I described the Lord's care for me with these words:

I have no way of counting how many cancer cells are active in my body. My oncologist tells me my particular kind of cancer recurs up to twenty years after its first appearance. During the months since surgery, I have sought the strength of my Shepherd often, for every day has been a walk of faith. Entering the sheepfold, I cupped my hands, needing to receive many gifts. Soon, however, I sensed my healing would come as I interceded for friends and acquaintances.

Medically I cannot verify the truth of that belief, yet spiritually and emotionally I can. As I pray for others, I open my arms to embrace them and their needs. Because of those arms flung wide, I receive still another gift. I see miracles happen, ones difficult to pray for, but easier to assess than my involvement with cancer. Each time I praise God for his answers to others it encourages me to believe for gifts I cannot see.

Faith Thought

"Ask, and it will be given you; seek and you will find; knock, and it will be opened to you. For every one who asks receives, and he who seeks finds, and to him who knocks it will be opened." (Matt. 7:7)

When I fall to my knees,
afraid of whatever darkness
surrounds me,
remind me, Jesus,
that you invite me
to come as a little child,
that you wrap your arms
around me,
yet also walk beside me,
holding my hand.

Thank you for going ahead,
leading me on
in whatever way I feel afraid.
I praise you, Jesus,
that life in you is abundant,
full of joy and surprises,
full of gifts I cannot yet see,
but most of all, full of you!

CHAPTER EIGHT

GOD'S REMEDY FOR PAIN

There's something harder
than dealing with physical cancer.
How can I cope with the way
other people treat me?
How can I handle the rumors,
hurt, and resentment I feel?

HE WAS HALF MY AGE, but taught me something important. When I said, "Phil, I'm sorry to hear that your dad died," he answered, "I really miss him. But I don't have the leftover baggage that so many people have when someone dies."

I've thought about Phil's words often. More than once, they have forced me to evaluate my relationships with others. I've needed to ask, "Am I carrying something that could become leftover baggage?"

During my first summer on chemotherapy, friends of ours loaned us their cabin for a week. As I sat on a deck overlooking the blue waters of a Minnesota lake, I faced reality. *My doctors tell me I might not live. Whichever way things go, I have a battle ahead of me. I don't want anything to slow me down.*

That meant I had to be honest with myself. Inside, I was a much bigger mess than I wanted to admit. What could the stress of bottled-up hurt and resentment do to my body? As I faced that question, I knew I had no choice but to deal with the hurts I had accumulated over a lifetime.

In giving us the Lord's prayer, Jesus offers a key for dealing with every relationship, whether human or divine. We begin by looking up into the face of our heavenly Father. If a woman has been abused, betrayed, or abandoned, that may be hard to do because of her association with an earthly father. But Pastor Michael Foss explains: "When Jesus teaches us to call God 'Father,' he is telling us that all human fathers are to be modeled after God—not the other way around." Mike points out that the role of human father is a privilege that bears the responsibility to reflect God's relationship with us and the world:

> *When Jesus tells us to call God "Our FATHER," he wants us to know that our God would be known to us as a loving parent. This is not a gender issue. Neither is this a power issue. The Savior tells us that the God of all creation and humanity desires an intimate relationship with us based upon trust and affection. This is an invitation from Jesus for us to picture crawling up into a beloved parent's lap, being wrapped in that parent's giving love, and feeling absolutely free to share whatever is in our hearts or minds with God.*

If we sense that we are looking up into the face of a loving parent, the rest of our conversation becomes completely different. Can you imagine how it might go? "You, Father—you who are in heaven. You who created the whole world, us included. We worship you, Father, and the minute we do, we stop looking at our problems and our own selves and focus on you.

"We worship you, because you are holy. We ask that your kingdom comes among us and that your will be done in our lives. We ask that each day you give us the bread we need. And forgive us our sins, for . . ."

For what? *"For we ourselves forgive everyone who is indebted to us"* (Luke 11:4).

Forgive everyone who owes us in some way because of what they have done to us? It's a debt, isn't it? If they've hurt us, they're indebted to us! Interesting, isn't it?

But then there's our end of it. It's hard to forgive. Forgiveness involves something that hurts us. How can we possibly forgive someone who has caused us deep pain?

When we forgive someone, it does not mean that what they did was right. Nor are we being passive, allowing anyone who wants to trample us underfoot to do so. Instead forgiveness is an indication of strength and courage. We do not want to be victims, but to bring change to what is happening to us.

Moreover, we understand that God's forgiveness of us is conditional on our willingness to forgive others. We choose to forgive the sins of others so that we ourselves might be forgiven.

In the weeks following surgery I learned that facing cancer is sometimes easier than dealing with the way people feel about cancer. In those years before open communication about breast cancer, I was treated so strangely that I began feeling that I had a communicable disease.

Immediately after returning home from the hospital, I asked for God's hedge of protection around me. At first that hedge offered the shelter I needed. As time went on, I heard so many rumors about myself that I just wanted to be left alone. That's a dangerous situation for anyone in crisis.

One day a pastor told me, "Lois, if you had lived in Bible times, your disease would have been leprosy."

To some people his words might sound negative. To me they offered comfort. While cancer and leprosy are definitely two different diseases, I could see a parallel in the way patients were sometimes treated. Though I hadn't read of anyone being healed of cancer in Scripture, it encouraged me to see lepers cleansed by the power of Christ's command.

Just the same, the reactions I received brought me to the point of asking my surgeon, "Do I have it right? That cancer isn't catching?"

He grinned. "You have it right, Lois." He nodded toward his office nurse. "What about Brenda? Before coming here she worked with dying patients for eight years. Where do you think she'd be?"

When I sensed that God wanted me to leave my protected home environment and return to speaking, I could no longer ignore the rumors. Within three months after my mastectomy I heard three separate tales about the funeral being planned for me. I felt it was all right if people buried me. I just thought I should die first. As one cancer patient said, "I started to feel I was disappointing people by not dying." Another told me, "They're calling me Lazarus, but I believe it's not yet my time to die." In a letter Mark Twain put it best of all: "Reports of my death are greatly exaggerated."

Thirteen months after surgery, a friend phoned. "Lois, I know this is silly when I just saw you last week. And I've known all along that you've had to deal with rumors. But today was the first time I heard one myself. I'm devastated. You really are getting along okay, aren't you?"

The rumors offered a constant threat to my morale. Always the stories were greatly exaggerated and often involved events that never happened to me. As I heard what people said, I began to think, "Well, maybe they're right. Maybe that *will* happen to me." Each time I allowed that thought, I felt smothered by a thick, dark cloud.

It was then I realized how dangerous rumors are. They threatened my will to live.

Inevitably these circumstances forced me into learning more about forgiveness. When something difficult happens, it's usually best to talk through a situation. Yet the widespread nature of the rumors made that impossible. I could not talk with each person who created or magnified stories about me. There were too many people involved. I couldn't even begin to guess who they were.

But Jesus said we need to forgive. *So there must be a way to do it*, I thought. Then I remembered the words of John 20:23: "If you forgive the sins of any, they are forgiven; if you retain the sins of any, they are retained."

Retained within me, I thought. *Kept within me. Bottled up where I can feel the hurt again and again.*

Unforgiven sins truly are retained—often in the habits of the person causing a wound. Retained also in those who are hurt, in terms of bitterness and resentment. When we delay our forgiveness, we retain the sins of others in the form of negative feelings. Our anger turns inward, and we grow increasingly resentful, bitter, and depressed.

Long before this happened, my dislike for gossip had been deep. Yet I had no choice but to forgive—that is, if I wanted to devote whatever strength I had to becoming well. Nor could I wait until I felt emotionally ready to forgive the people who had hurt me. That day would probably never come.

"I *want* to forgive," I started to pray, but knew that wouldn't do it.

"I *choose* to forgive," I prayed instead. "Right now. In this moment. Whether I like it or not."

It was not a bigger-than-life moment. I was just a human being guessing at the power in one secret: that if I forgave as Jesus told me to forgive, I would find a way to go on. I discovered another life principle:

> *When we choose to forgive, we*
> *release God's power and take*
> *hold of his remedy for pain.*

After my prayer I felt peaceful. The rumors no longer mattered. I had forgiven the people involved. I simply wanted to go on.

In the years since, I've returned to the John 20:23 concept countless times, simply praying, "Lord Jesus, in your name I forgive the person who hurt me. I ask you to bless that person. Remove the hurt, resentment, bitterness, and any other negative feelings I have. In your name I ask for your healing."

When we choose to forgive, good feelings may not come with our first prayer. Good feelings may not come until we've offered that prayer twenty, or fifty, or one hundred times. If my hurt returns, I simply repeat that prayer or say, "Jesus, in your name I *have* forgiven the person involved." If needed, I speak my prayer aloud to make it seem more real. Yet God hears every one of us the first time, because we pray with our will, according to his command. At the right moment he creates the change, giving us the needed feelings.

Once we have forgiven, we have the privilege of asking God to restore wholeness—to give healing of emotions, intellect, spirit, and body. When we are honest in asking, the Lord is faithful in answering. He doesn't waste pain.

After years of buried hurt and a long stint on chemotherapy, one woman prayed about the husband from whom she had been divorced early in life. As she finished praying, tears of relief ran down her cheeks. "I knew I had to take care of it!" she exclaimed. "I knew I had to forgive. But I didn't know how because he died long ago." Subsequently her good health was confirmed by doctors.

Through forgiveness, I release not only my feelings but also the person or individuals involved. In the John 20:23 prayer I say, "Lord, I want to do all that I can, humanly speaking. In your name I forgive that person." Offering such a prayer recognizes Christ's greater power and is a way of asking, "Remove the chains of what that person did against me. I want you to have the freedom to work in that individual's life." That doesn't mean that *all* the chains in a person's life are removed. That person may have hurt others also. But I'm only responsible for the bondage that involves me.

After I mentioned my experience with this prayer, a woman attending one of my seminars told how John 20:23 had helped her. Several years before, Britta had heard a speaker tell about a banner someone made for him. The word *forgiveness* had been broken up, giving it added meaning: "I am for giving life to others."

Britta explained, "As we forgive, God forgives us and gives new life. As we forgive others, we in turn loosen them from the bondage of our unforgiving spirit, giving them the possibility of new life in the Lord."

A public school teacher, Britta had a girl named Amy in a twelfth-grade class. Because of a decision that Britta later realized was wrong, a personality conflict developed between her and Amy. Though unable to keep Amy in class, Britta continued to pray for her. Britta and another teacher became prayer partners, joined at times by friends. That year they prayed for Amy and other students.

After graduation, Amy left town, but the Holy Spirit continued to remind Britta to intercede for her. "Years later, when cleaning out a drawer, I found several derogatory notes Amy had written. Remembering John 20:23, about binding people with our unforgiving spirits, I tore up the notes, claiming aloud forgiveness for Amy in Jesus' name. About two weeks later I was at school getting ready for a new year when Amy came to see me.

"Looking at her, I realized something had happened. She had become a Christian—such a radiant, changed girl that I knew what the expression 'born again' meant." Though Britta does not consider herself a hugging person, she and Amy hugged that day. Love had been released, a natural outcome of forgiveness.

In *The Promise of the Spirit* William Barclay writes, "We should realize the reason for so many of our failures in the work of Christ, if we remembered that where there are broken personal relationships the Spirit cannot come."

As I faced the rumor problem, praying forgiveness with my will, God stepped in, gradually changing my inner self. While replacing hurt and resentment, he gave me a sense of humor about the situation that became resurrection power. Finally I prayed, "Lord, take the rumors and use them for your honor and glory. You know who the rumor makers are. I don't. Use my illness in a special way with each of them."

Soon I sensed something different in groups to which I spoke. At times I guessed there were people who came out of curiosity. Yet I also saw the Lord at work, using what I had experienced as an opportunity to help people see him.

FAITH THOUGHT

BEAR WITH EACH OTHER AND FORGIVE WHATEVER GRIEV-
ANCE YOU MAY HAVE AGAINST ONE ANOTHER. FORGIVE AS
THE LORD FORGAVE YOU. (COL. 3:13 NIV)

Lord Jesus,
in those moments
when I want to weep
and cannot,
give me the willingness—
even more,
the grace and courage—
to forgive,
talk with,
pray for,
and then love
those who have hurt me.

Thanks, Lord,
that if I let you,
you will make me new.
I'm grateful
that all the things
I cannot do myself
become possible
through
your resurrection power.
Help me begin, Jesus.
Then help me continue.

CHAPTER NINE

WORDS THAT GIVE US LIFE

—◆●◆—

*I want to go on
to wholeness.
Will you tell me more?*

As I REALIZED THE DIFFERENCE the John 20:23 prayer made in my life, I began asking Jesus to heal me of any past emotional baggage that made me excessively sensitive. I hoped to give him the opportunity to make my morale the best it could be.

Off and on during that week of vacation at the Minnesota cabin, God reminded me of ways in which I had been hurt. Now that I had the key for what I should do, I thought back to different segments of my life, praying with my will each time the Holy Spirit brought a difficult situation to mind. I learned those words so well I could repeat them in my sleep: "Lord Jesus, in your name I forgive the person who hurt me. I ask you to bless that person. Forgive me for any resentment, or bitterness, or hurt that I feel. Remove those feelings from me and give me your healing."

Repeatedly I sensed a healing peace and knew that situation had been taken care of. But at last the Spirit reminded me of a situation about which I prayed, and forgave, and did *not* sense peace. When that memory from seventeen years before kept returning, I finally prayed, "Jesus, if you want me to talk with that person, I'm willing."

By then I didn't even know where the person I'll call Rosemary lived. But God knew. Shortly after we returned home from vacation, I received a phone call from her. "Lois, I'll be passing through town, and I'm wondering if we could get together."

A few weeks later I met Rosemary for lunch. With the maturity that comes with time, I realized how much I had hurt her seventeen years before. I knew there was an area of her life in which she would not go on unless I asked forgiveness. And I knew that's what God expected me to do.

If we wait until we feel emotionally ready to forgive, we will never do it. Think about another life principle:

> *Forgiveness and blessing are given or withheld*
> *through a decision. With our free will we decide*
> *whether to keep our pain or to receive healing.*

"How many times should I forgive my brother?" Peter asked. "Up to seven times?" "Not seven times," Jesus told him, "but seventy-seven times" (Matt. 18:21-22).

I suspect Jesus knew that our relationships with relatives, friends, and coworkers can be most difficult. Why else would we continue seeing a person after being hurt countless times? Usually our need to forgive intertwines with our need to communicate. So how do we begin?

Recognize the Opportunity

At eighteen years of age, a woman I'll call Sandra married a person she believed to be a nice, churchgoing boy. Soon after, she learned her husband had spent several years in a federal penitentiary for manslaughter and had been released as incorrigible. Eventually he was diagnosed as having a sociopathic personality.

Sandra and her children experienced his problems in the form of violence and abuse. Never was there enough money for basic necessities. In spite of his marital infidelities and frequent abandonments, she stayed with him. When she was pregnant with their third child, Gary left for the last time.

Because of the abusive situation in which Sandra lived for some time, she could have remained a victim. Instead as a new Christian, she wanted to do some spiritual housecleaning—to forgive not only her former husband but also *every* person and circumstance that had hurt her. She explained: "I made a list of all the real and imagined offences committed against me. Then I burned it. When the list went up in flames and became ashes, it could not be brought back together in its original form. In the same way, as I forgave, the offenses against me were gone. They didn't exist anymore."

When we delay forgiveness, our anger and other negative feelings become harmful to us and the people around us. They often become toxic and taint everything we do.

Take Responsibility

More than once I've needed to listen to my self-talk. If I hear myself saying, "Yes, but . . ." I know there's something I really don't want to change. I see only problems, not possibilities.

"When Jesus controls a life, excuses stop," said one young woman. "All the wrong things happened to me. I put the blame on others. But spring came to my life when I realized I could take responsibility. I can make a difference in what happens to me."

Jesus wants to give each of us the power to deal with a situation openly. If we take care of something at once, we save ourselves years of pain and accumulated hurt. I've learned the hard way that if I've done something wrong I might as well apologize right away: "I'm sorry I did that. I'm sorry for the hurt I've caused. Will you forgive me?"

Countless times the person involved has answered, "Of course I forgive you. And you know, I did such and such. I'm sorry about that. Will you forgive *me*?" They've acted relieved that someone made the first move to set things right. Whenever that happens I feel as if I've gained a new friend.

Other times people have said, "You know there really isn't anything to forgive. But if it helps you, I *do* give forgiveness. I want you to know everything is okay between us."

Only once have I received an even deeper wound. When I asked forgiveness, the person replied, "Yes, I forgive you. But you also did this, and this, and this." To each wrong, whether real or imagined, I answered, "Will you forgive me for that also?" Finally I could bear no more and quietly finished the conversation.

As soon as I was alone the tears came—a torrent of them. When I dried my swollen eyes, I realized something had changed—not in the person, but in me. I had always thought, *It's all my fault. If I keep trying, I can make the situation right. Our relationship will be perfect.* That day God used the situation to get rid of my false guilt. He removed my feelings of rejection, giving me the sense, "You've done your best. It's in my hands."

God redeemed that situation in which I probably allowed myself to be more trampled on than necessary. The Lord knew my heart and brought ultimate good. But let's take another look at the whole problem.

When my husband experienced anticipatory grief, he realized that he also needed to forgive other difficult circumstances. Counselor Vernon Bittner gave Roy a crucial reminder:

> What if you resent the way someone treated you, and you ask forgiveness, but they won't forgive you? That makes you dependent for your forgiveness upon them. We need to forgive; that's why it's important for us to say to people, "I forgive you for what you've done to me." But we actually don't need anyone's forgiveness except God's. The Lord's prayer says, "Forgive us our sins as we forgive those who sin against us."

Even if someone else doesn't know how to respond by giving forgiveness, we can fulfill our part by saying and meaning, "I forgive you."

Change the Pattern

A friend I'll call Marla talked about a long-standing grievance at work. "I felt I should go to Bill, my supervisor, and say, 'I forgive you,' even though he didn't realize there was a need for forgiveness. But I certainly argued with God. I didn't *want* to go. Then I sensed his prompting: 'Do it anyway, even if you don't feel like it.'

"I thought I had forgiven and received healing before, but this time it was as if the healing was complete. Later on, another person was upset with Bill and came to me, wanting to complain. I told the person, 'I'm sorry. Bill and I have reconciled, and I can't break that reconciliation.'"

When forgiveness occurs, it's important that the man or woman who is wronged sees the person who did the wrong as someone who is cleansed by Jesus Christ and forgiven by him. If that does not happen, it's as though the person wronged expects to be wronged again. Men who have been unfaithful to their wives sometimes say, "My wife said she forgave me, but she treated me as though she expected me to be unfaithful again. I started wondering if I should meet that expectation."

Restored relationships come when forgiveness restores dignity to the person who did wrong. Richard Hanson puts it well: "Real forgiveness requires a resolution of all feelings to the point of equal honor for both parties. Both must see each other as worthy and good. They must part with equal dignity. True forgiveness leaves the offender with as much innocence as the offended."

To restore dignity to another, we may need to sacrifice our desire to win. As one friend put it, "I don't have to be Mrs. Right on every occasion." She wanted the forgiven person to be her friend, not someone who would always be uncomfortable with her.

Forgive and Forget?

But what happens if we truly are not able to trust the person we have forgiven? God does not expect us to continue to submit to something that has the potential to cause great emotional, spiritual, and physical harm. There are times when it's essential that we forgive with our eyes open. Usually those are the situations where we need the help of a strong Christian counselor.

By contrast, what about other kinds of situations where we are not talking about ongoing abuse? "I can pray and forgive," said one woman. "But I find it much harder to forget."

When someone has hurt us deeply, I personally don't believe it's possible to forget. But we can receive a level of healing in which we remember what happened but are free of pain.

To my surprise, that freedom came as I learned still another step in prayer. Sometimes I'm able to pray for someone who hurt me only by allowing the Spirit to pray through me. In those moments I turn over my inadequate human love and ask, "Lord, give me your love, so it can flow through me to the person for whom I pray. Give me your words."

In those moments I discover the possibility of what Christ taught when he said: "Love your enemies, bless them that curse you, do good to them that hate you, and pray for them which despitefully use you and persecute you" (Matt. 5:44 KJV).

For me that means taking practical steps. The first is to pray the John 20:23 prayer, forgiving the person and asking in the name of Jesus for his blessing on the person who wounded me. After such a prayer, I usually sense peace. If the enemy who is our accuser returns to remind me of a hurtful situation, I try to remember to pray, "In the name of Jesus, I *have* forgiven that person." Instead of arguing with the accuser, I repeat a verse of Scripture, aloud if needed.

I've discovered that if I pray for the person who hurt me, I apparently make the accuser very unhappy. It's the best way I know to stop him reminding me of a person I don't want to think about.

When I pray in this way, I need to remember that my petitions do not go directly from me to the person for whom I intercede. Prayers travel from me, to God (and thankfully, he can refine them), then to the other person. As one woman wrote, "Jesus Christ knew what he was talking about when He advised us to pray for our enemies. He was no idealist. He was the world's most uncompromising realist. He knew that when we become so completely immersed in God that we can actually pray for those who hate us and despitefully use us, then His power flows through us so strongly that we can ask what we will and it shall be done unto us."

Someone has said they never prayed for a person without learning to love them. I agree. Nor have I prayed without learning startling things about myself. Once the discovery took six months. Each day I pleaded for a moody, cantankerous man with whom I worked, "Lord, may he become a Christian." It took a long time to realize I wanted that man to receive salvation so he would be nicer to me. In a heart-searing moment of truth, a new prayer tumbled out, "God, forgive and change me." Only after that man saw something different in me did he begin to change.

If we wish to recover from a deep injury, we have no choice but to forgive. People often say, "You know, I need inner healing." All of us need inner healing for one reason or another, but let's understand what it really is. We miss the point of what Jesus said if we fail to focus on his redemptive work, his ability to rid us of rage, guilt, fear, helplessness, and a negative self-image.

Mary Ehrlichmann, mother of five, knows what it means to forgive in spite of excruciating pain. Her schoolteacher husband, Don, and their nineteen-year-old son, Michael, tried to help three Minneapolis boys because they seemed to need a friend. Within twenty minutes Don was dead, shot three times as he diverted attention from Michael.

At the memorial service another son, twenty-four-year-old Jim, expressed the thoughts of the family:

Peace, reconciliation, salvation will not be brought about by
bloodshed, murder, by laws, by revenge, by hate returned for hate.
No, God prescribes only one remedy for our situation—love! If
we want an end to the kind of thing which struck my dad down,
then God says this is the only way—love! It is the demand of
the Gospel and God is plenty serious about it. . . .

    My friends, it is not enough to believe in God. We must also
believe in his way of doing things, we must believe in love and
take it upon ourselves, no matter what the cost, to bring this love
to a world which desperately needs it now. My family and I
intend to honor the memory of our dad and his faith by seeking
the strength to accomplish this goal. I pray that you will con-
sider the same. May God help us.

When asked to explain the spirit of joy within her home
the day after the funeral, Mary said, "It's the grace of God." In
an open letter published in Jim Klobuchar's column in the
Minneapolis *Star*, Mary wrote to the boys who murdered her
husband:

My thoughts keep turning to you three. You may feel that you are
men, but to me you are just boys—like my own sons—and I
wonder to whom you are turning for comfort and strength and
reassurance. . . .

    Know that God forgives you and that my family and I for-
give you—then go out and make something worthwhile of the
rest of your lives. . . .

    God keep and bless you.

Years later Mary explained to a church group: "Resentment, bitterness, lack of forgiveness, these cancers consume
not the objects toward which they are directed; they consume
the hosts. People know baseball is the New York Yankees' *game*.
They should know forgiveness isn't the Christian's *game*. It's
our *uniqueness*. . . . My spirit could not have survived the dou-
ble burden of grief and hatred."

"I believe that the only unimpeachable mark of the indwelling power of the Holy Spirit is love," writes Robert C. Tuttle Jr. in an article in *Face to Face:* "When the Holy Spirit enters our lives, we not only have power to love but power to overcome life's problems, power to propel us beyond the level of mere existence, power to teach these whirlwinds in which we live how to dance."

After seeing her beloved sister Betsie die in a concentration camp, Corrie ten Boom was miraculously released. In *The Hiding Place,* a book coauthored with John and Elizabeth Sherrill, Corrie tells about an experience at the end of World War II. As she spoke to a group in Munich, one of her jailers, an SS man at Ravensbruck, came forward. "How grateful I am for your message, Fraulein," he said. "To think that, as you say, He has washed my sins away!"

Corrie gives her reaction:

His hand was thrust out to shake mine. And I, who had preached so often to the people in Bloemendaal the need to forgive, kept my hand at my side.

Even as the angry, vengeful thoughts boiled through me, I saw the sin of them. Jesus Christ had died for this man; was I going to ask for more? Lord Jesus, I prayed, forgive me and help me to forgive him.

I tried to smile, I struggled to raise my hand. I could not. I felt nothing, not the slightest spark of warmth or charity. And so again I breathed a silent prayer. Jesus, I cannot forgive him. Give me Your forgiveness.

As I took his hand the most incredible thing happened. From my shoulder along my arm and through my hand a current seemed to pass from me to him, while into my heart sprang a love for this stranger that almost overwhelmed me.

And so I discovered that it is not on our forgiveness any more than on our goodness that the world's healing hinges, but on His. When He tells us to love our enemies, He gives, along with the command, the love itself.

Amazing, isn't it? Forgiveness given becomes forgiveness, love, and healing received.

FAITH THOUGHT

"A NEW COMMANDMENT I GIVE TO YOU, THAT YOU LOVE ONE ANOTHER; EVEN AS I HAVE LOVED YOU, THAT YOU ALSO LOVE ONE ANOTHER. BY THIS ALL MEN WILL KNOW THAT YOU ARE MY DISCIPLES, IF YOU HAVE LOVE FOR ONE ANOTHER." (JOHN 13:34-35)

Yes, Jesus, it's true
that when I refuse to forgive
I retain those sins within me.
Help me to deal with
whatever is causing a problem.
I accept responsibility
for my share of that problem
and ask you to forgive me.
In your name, Jesus,
and by the power of your Spirit,
I forgive and ask you to bless
the person or people
who have hurt me.
I praise you, Jesus,
that when I forgive in your name
you speak to my mind,
emotions, and spirit,
giving your healing
and peace. Thank you!

You Can Hear the Voice of God

———◆●◆———

Sometimes I wish
I could look down from heaven,
seeing things
from God's big, overall view.
What is he trying to tell me?
How can I know?

YOU FEEL CONFUSED, LACKING DIRECTION, or you hurt and
need comfort. You're anxious, filled with fear, or wondering
if your prayers are being heard. Perhaps you're even saying, "I'm
not sure if it's the Lord speaking or just me making things up.
How can I know if I'm hearing him?"

Not long ago I realized that though I had tried to reach several people, I had not heard a human voice in two days. Auto-
mated answering systems, yes, with complicated mazes: "If you
want this, press this number," and the endless trail that followed.
Voice mail, yes. E-mail, yes. But not a single, unrecorded voice.

In times of suffering there are few things more difficult than
being ignored or finding only impersonal responses. Yet in what
can be a nameless mass of humanity, our Lord promises that he
knows us as individuals and that we belong to him.

What did Jesus mean when he said, "My sheep hear my voice, and I know them, and they follow me" (John 10:27)? Is his voice an audible one? The Bible tells us about times when people *do* hear God's voice, but he's not limited to that. Instead if we are willing to listen, he speaks to us with unending variety and creativity.

While not attempting to limit God, I find it helpful to be aware of different ways he moves on our behalf. When we seek him, it's easy to think that the only answer we want to receive is yes to whatever we ask. However, I've prayed long enough to be grateful for times God answers no. He also responds in ways that indicate *Wait for personal growth or better timing,* or, on occasion, *Get up and get going.*

This last response does not mean striving to answer my own prayers. One woman prayed, "Lord, give my daughter a good husband," and then systematically introduced her to every eligible male in the state. When God says, "Get up and get going," it does not mean we should force what we want to happen.

The Lord offers several means through which we hear his voice and then provides corresponding checkpoints. As we sense his will, these guidelines and checkpoints flow together, confirming one another.

Scripture

Our most important resource for hearing God is his written Word. When I faced cancer, my needs were so great that I longed for the sound of my Shepherd's voice. In every crisis, reason for fear, or need for guidance, I wanted to turn to the Lord. I needed his viewpoint, not just my own. I learned to start my daily Scripture reading with a prayer: "Lord, what do you want me to know?" (see chapter 3).

Numerous passages of guidance came just as I needed them. Eight months after my mastectomy, I received special encouragement. My oncologist told me he would change my chemotherapy to a different combination of drugs. I had mixed reactions—partially good, for doctors had found the program offered better results than the regimen I had been on. Also, if I did not suffer a recurrence in the meantime, I might finish treatments at the end of ten more months.

For the first time I received the hope that I might go off chemotherapy instead of being on it the rest of my life. Even so, I dreaded the unknowns, the injections, the possibility of additional side effects. But then the morning I was to begin the new treatment, my reading included Psalm 27:13-14: "I believe that I shall see the goodness of the Lord in the land of the living! Wait for the Lord; be strong, and let your heart take courage; yea, wait for the Lord!"

Each of us who faces a difficult situation is in a good position to hear from the Lord. The more empty we are, the more willing we are to listen. We receive encouragement and guidance from the Lord in direct proportion to how dependent we are on him. We come to that dependence when we believe that God means what he says. Those things forbidden in the Word of God are forbidden. Those things regarded as holy are holy.

When we recognize the divine inspiration and authority of Scripture, we also believe that God does not lie. He leads in ways that are consistent with his character (Heb. 6:17-20). Out of that comes our first checkpoint: *All guidance, encouragement, or answers to prayer should be found in Scripture or be consistent with its overall body of truth.*

As we seek guidance, it's important to ask, "What kind of passage is the Holy Spirit making real to me right now?" When we know that, we have a solid beginning for hearing God's voice in both immediate and long-term ways.

Again, there's a life principle involved:

> *If we seek God honestly*
> *and are willing to listen,*
> *we find him ready to speak.*

If we consistently read the Bible, we give the Holy Spirit the opportunity to spotlight groups of verses in the way John Sherrill mentioned (see chapter 3). Often he teaches us through a verse or passage. Other times he brings alive topics of which we need understanding. Over time he seems to arrange our personal schooling by showing us what Scripture says about perseverance, forgiveness, prayer, or healing. When we need direction, he gladly gives it.

Inward Assurance

When I seek God's leading, I often receive guidance from Scripture first. On other occasions I sense an inward assurance that is then confirmed through Scripture. Many Christians describe this inward leading as something Elijah knew after a time of discouragement (1 Kings 19:12-13). The Lord was not in a powerful storm that shattered rocks and tore the mountains apart. The Lord was not in an earthquake, nor in a fire. But God spoke to Elijah in a still, small voice that told him what to do next.

Many Christians describe that still, small voice as something coming from deep within. Through a gentle whisper, God shows his concern for us and the details of our lives. In communist countries the Holy Spirit has led Christians step-by-step to the house of strangers. There they found refuge with other Christians. During times of persecution, the Spirit has also set places and hours of meeting. Every believer in the group was present.

Since it's possible to hear from both God and Satan, it's important to remember a checkpoint—the prayer, "*Lord, if this thought is of you, increase it; if not, remove it.*"

At one point I felt bombarded by reminders of a certain couple. No matter what I was doing, I started thinking about them. Whenever that happens, I want to know if I'm hearing God or if Satan is trying to distract me. I test it out by praying for the person about whom I'm reminded. I pay special attention to reminders that increase as I pray. Sometimes God leads me to write and ask how they are doing. In this instance I felt I should call. I discovered that the husband had been involved in a life-threatening accident.

Another means of inward assurance is a deep inner knowing. Think of Paul saying, "I know whom I have believed" (2 Tim. 1:12). When Christians are asked, "Explain what you mean by knowing," they often reply, "I can't describe it. I just *know*." Perhaps *certainty* would be a good word—a deep inward certainty. Before I married Roy, I felt absolutely certain that God wanted him to be my husband.

Many Christians also receive a nudging to do something or leave it undone. Scripture doesn't tell us why Mary went to visit Elizabeth. I suspect that the Holy Spirit gave Mary an "I ought to" feeling. She was blessed by her cousin's response.

When speaking to us through an inward assurance, God sometimes gives a sense of urgency that it's time to act. Often the inward nudges of the Spirit prompt something that seems natural to do. You might be led to mow the lawn of an elderly neighbor without knowing she has been praying about that need. Or you may sense that you should call a friend, as I did. If this urgency is God given, you generally will not know peace until you act on what he tells you. Although these actions seem like everyday things to do, the person on the receiving end often understands that something special has happened. God has moved you to act on another person's behalf.

Other times we may be prompted to do something that seems more unusual. The day before one of our sons graduated from high school, I kept sensing that I should stop cleaning and go to a hardware store to buy kerosene lamps. I thought, *That's really strange. We don't need kerosene lamps.* But after several nudges I obeyed.

I discovered some really good lamps on a closeout sale. The moment I bought them I felt peace. I brought them home and put them away, still not understanding my need for them. But the need came when our earning power was stretched to the limit, and Roy and I lived for most of the summer without electricity.

Our ability to hear the Spirit's voice and recognize his leading grows with experience. If you wonder whether the Lord is asking you to do something, consider the question that is another checkpoint: *"Am I being led to do something that is consistent with Christ's love for all people?"* An action not in keeping with God's command to love one another is not his leading.

God also gives inward assurance through dreams and visions. Through the prophet Joel, the Lord promised, "And it shall come to pass afterward, that I will pour out my spirit on all flesh; your sons and your daughters shall prophesy, your old men shall dream dreams, and your young men shall see visions" (Joel 2:28).

How do you distinguish between a dream and a vision? A person receives a dream while sleeping and a vision while awake. Often the person receiving a vision has been praying, alone or with a group of praying and worshiping believers. More than once my husband has received a vision while listening to Christian music. Sometimes a dream or vision offers inward assurance to the person who receives it. Other times dreams and visions confirm the leading of other people.

Both John and Peter received visions while praying. As a prisoner on the island of Patmos, John wrote, "I was in the Spirit on the Lord's day, and I heard behind me a loud voice like a trumpet saying, 'Write what you see in a book and send it to the seven churches . . .'" (Rev. 1:10-11). The vision that followed became the book of Revelation. From Peter's vision on the rooftop came the giving of the gospel to the Gentiles (Acts 10:9—11:18).

Soon after the birth of Christ, Joseph was warned in a dream to take the baby and Mary to Egypt (Matt. 2:13). So great was the urgency of the message that Joseph did not wait for morning but acted immediately.

A Christian I know received a dream so powerful that she remembered every detail. Not long after, she again experienced almost the identical dream. Then, in her morning devotions, the Holy Spirit made real the words of Joseph of Egypt: "The doubling of Pharaoh's dream means that the thing is fixed by God, and God will shortly bring it to pass" (Gen. 41:32).

Within a three-week period, from people unknown to one another and living far apart, I heard two other versions of the same dream. In each the symbol was different, but the message was identical: a warning of difficult times, but "Keep your eyes on the Lord, and he will take you through."

More than once I've longed to receive a dream or vision from the Lord. So far my dreams have come after a meal of fatty foods, onion rings, or chocolate cake. By contrast, I truly listen when my husband describes something he has received. God has given him both dreams and visions that offered specific leading or comfort about something we needed to know.

In this, too, we have a checkpoint: *Ask the Lord if a vision or dream is from him and, if so, to confirm it in another way.* Unless you hear as well and as urgently as Joseph, the husband of Mary, and Joseph of Egypt, wait for that confirmation before making a life-changing decision.

Few of us believe that we never make a mistake in recognizing what the Lord is trying to tell us. The problem isn't with God's ability to speak. If there's a communication problem, it's usually because we haven't taken the time to listen.

During the last winter of my father's life I wanted to spend as much time as possible with him. Mom had died the previous July, and in addition to dealing with his illness, Dad was lonely. Yet it was sixty miles one way to his nursing home, and our Minnesota roads can be treacherous in winter. Even if I started out in good weather, it sometimes changed dramatically by the time I returned home.

I learned to pray for openings in the weather that would provide a safe trip out and back, as well as time with Dad. But late one afternoon as I entered the freeway, heading south for my return trip, it started to rain. My stomach tightened. I had no doubt what that meant.

Within another ten miles the rain changed to icy pellets clattering against the windshield. I turned on the radio: "Ice storm with rapidly deteriorating conditions blankets the entire metro area." Inwardly I groaned. I was out in the country at the north end of Minneapolis and St. Paul, heading south. I needed to pass all the way through the cities to reach our home at the southern end.

Swallowing hard, I began to pray. Within another five miles

the road collected icy patches. As the cars around me slowed up, I gradually dropped back, giving myself extra space between vehicles. Watching the exits, I started searching for a restaurant or a place where I could stay overnight, if necessary. Just then a car whizzed past me, fishtailed three or four times, and regained control. I tried to breathe deeply, but my hands clenched the steering wheel.

Then, a few miles north of the 694 beltway that arcs around Minneapolis and St. Paul, I sensed an inner whisper. *Take 694 east.*

"694?" I asked, sure that I was hearing wrong. I never went that way. Taking the freeway straight through St. Paul was much more direct.

Again I sensed that inner whisper. *Take 694 east.*

By the time I reached the interchange, the entire freeway I was on had glazed over. Even the most careless drivers had slowed down. Again I wondered if I wanted a much longer trip. Once more I prayed and felt that was God's direction.

I pulled off on an icy exit ramp and crawled onto 694 east. Within one mile the sleet stopped pelting my windshield. Within two miles I saw the road was not only free of ice, but the pavement was dry.

It hasn't rained here? I couldn't believe my eyes.

Soon the treacherous conditions only a few miles back seemed like another world. All the way home I drove on dry pavement. As I swung around the metro area, then dropped south again, I felt as if I were living a dream, held in the protective hand of God. Only as I pulled into our driveway did a wet, slippery snow begin.

Even now, after following the Lord for many years, I don't always recognize his long view. Sometimes I'm too close to even see his day-to-day leading. But when I recognize it for what it is, I stand back in awe. I know God has given me yet another reason to trust in his ultimate plan.

FAITH THOUGHT

THUS SAYS THE LORD: "STAND BY THE ROADS, AND LOOK,
AND ASK FOR THE ANCIENT PATHS, WHERE THE GOOD WAY
IS; AND WALK IN IT, AND FIND REST FOR YOUR SOULS."
(JER. 6:16)

Strange, Lord,
I thought I had to walk alone
against the driving sleet
of pain, discouragement, and fear—
yet alleluia!
Even as I felt
the cold bite of winter
you were there—
warming and guiding me,
caring for me with your presence.

Thank you, Lord,
for your still, small voice,
for your inward assurance
showing me what I need to know.
Each time I wonder if you understand
my needs, help me remember
that your love and peace
become mine with a thankful heart.

GOING BEYOND CONFUSION

Confused? Yes,
and needing direction
that takes me beyond
all the things that distract me.
How can God help me
sort out my confusion?

L ONG AGO, JONATHAN LIVED IN A CONFUSING SITUATION. His father, King Saul, wanted to kill his best friend, David. Jonathan knew that someday David would gain the throne that seemingly should have been his. How could he be loyal both to his father and to David? Holding the power of life or death, Jonathan stood between the two.

What could have been a terrible situation, tearing Jonathan into a thousand shreds, seemed no problem for him. What enabled him to live, apparently having no false guilt or jealousy but instead an amazing loyalty to David? Jonathan knew the mind of the Lord. Out of that he interceded for David.

Knowing the mind of God is another way of saying that Jonathan heard God's voice and sensed his will. The more difficult our situation, the more desperately every one of us needs to know the Lord's presence and leading. But how can this big God who created the entire universe provide details specifically tailored for us?

More than once Jesus called himself a shepherd. In contrast to the hired person who runs at the first sign of danger, the shepherd who owns his sheep cares in every way about their well-being. When he approaches the sheepfold, the shepherd whistles a tune or behaves in a way that is usual and familiar. He wants to be sure that his sheep know that he is the one who is coming. He even protects them from confusion. There's another life principle involved:

> *Under God's gracious leading, confusion*
> *offers the potential for certainty in him.*

Through Scripture and inward assurance we form a belief of what God wants us to know. Then he may use one or more of the following means to strengthen and confirm that guidance.

Righteous Counsel

Solomon said, "Where there is no guidance, a people falls; but in an abundance of counselors there is safety" (Prov. 11:14). Yet it depends on who those counselors are. A large group of unwise friends could encourage a teenager to do something that resulted in lifelong grief. By contrast, counselors should be mature in the Christian faith and have insight about God's long-term, overall plan for his people.

When seeking counsel, consider a checkpoint: *Ask God for counselors who see your situation from his viewpoint, not just their own.* Then, as you think about what they tell you, ask yourself:

Do I sense peace about following the ideas suggested?

Would that counsel ultimately bring life, though at first I drag my feet or don't want to forgive someone?

Is the counsel given consistent with the principles of Scripture?

Is it consistent with God's overall dealing in my life?

If counseling runs contrary to biblical truth, it's time to use your gift of discernment. You need someone who understands godly principles, as well as how he leads and guides individuals. When Jesus told his disciples that he had to go to Jerusalem to suffer and die, Peter lacked perception about Christ's earthly mission. He rebuked Christ, saying, "God forbid, Lord! This shall never happen to you." But Jesus said to Peter, "Get behind me, Satan! You are a hindrance to me; for you are not on the side of God, but of men" (Matt. 16:21-23).

Though we need discernment about choosing a counselor, we should also guard against being so critical that we don't receive needed counseling. Consider another checkpoint: *"Am I willing to talk about this situation with the right person? If not, why not?"* You may need to ask, "What am I ashamed of? What am I trying to hide? What am I uneasy about?"

In order to play fair with counselors, it's important to be honest about *all* the crucial details of the problem we bring to them. It's easy to withhold part of the story—especially any part that makes us uncomfortable. If counselors don't know such details, we're handing them a puzzle with three or four pieces missing. By withholding important information, we may be asking them to say yes to something we've already decided rightly or wrongly to do.

Peace or Uneasiness

My friend Catharine offered a wise guideline: "There's one thing that Satan can't imitate—the peace of God in your heart."

How can we describe that kind of peace? Perhaps it's easier to say what is *not* peace. Think about how you feel when there's a telephone ringing and no one picks it up. That sense of jangling inside you is the opposite of God's peace.

If you're having difficulty making an important decision, there's a test that can help you know whether to go ahead. It should not be used on something such as marriage, where it's necessary to know *without doubt* what to do. Instead this test might be helpful in deciding about a job, the sale of a home, or the course of your medical treatment.

First, define the decision you need to make. Narrow that decision down to two clear-cut choices, A and B. Write down those choices. List the good points, then the disadvantages, under each.

Then pray something like this: "Lord, to the best of my ability I believe you want me to make a certain choice. [Let's say A.] That's what I plan to do." While thinking that way, continue to pray for a period of time, perhaps three days or a week. If you sense peace and the timing is right, it may be all right for you to go ahead.

If, instead, you lack peace, go back to the place where you believe you made a wrong decision. Tell the Lord, "I'm going to take choice B instead." Again, pray for a time. If you sense peace in what you're planning, continue in the belief that you understand God's will.

Once you receive leading through peace and the other ways I've already mentioned, don't keep changing your mind unless God clearly gives you new information. If you keep flipping back and forth, you'll become like a wave of the sea, unstable in all you do.

Paul wrote, "The peace that Christ gives is to guide you in the decisions you make" (Col. 3:15 TEV). This peace is an inward sense that comes in spite of circumstances and offers another checkpoint: *If you lack peace, do not go ahead with doing something.*

Confirming Circumstances

Think about the specific clue with which God announced the birth of his Son: "And this will be a sign for you: you will find a babe wrapped in swaddling cloths and lying in a manger" (Luke 2:12). There weren't too many babies lying in a manger! God also gives signs to encourage our faith (2 Kings 20:1-11).

The Lord does not want us to refuse his signs because of unbelief (Isa. 7:10-17). Nor does he want us to use signs as a way of testing him (Exod. 17:1-7). If, instead, we seek God with a humble, open attitude, he will bless our honest request for help. That need gives us another checkpoint: *If you are unsure whether you're hearing God correctly, it is not a lack of faith to ask him to confirm something in an outward way.* When Gideon needed to be sure he was to lead the Israelites into battle, the Lord blessed his need for guidance (Judg. 6:17-18, 36-40).

Signs that follow prayer about a specific need might involve circumstances that are open doors. Not every opportunity is an open door. High school graduates, for instance, may have such a variety of opportunities that a choice seems overwhelming. Instead an open door follows specific prayer and circumstances that fall into a step-by-step pattern. These circumstances are arranged so perfectly that only God could be responsible.

The psalmist tells us, "The steps of a good man are ordered by the Lord" (Ps. 37:23 KJV). So are the stops! When we sense that ordering, we need to go as far ahead as God directs. When he wants us to go on, he arranges circumstances so we can act on them. Our circumstances might not be as dramatic as the wind blowing all night, creating a dry path for the Israelites to cross the Red Sea. Yet they will be just as real, for God still actively leads.

A skeptic might refer to God's ordering of circumstances by saying, "That's a coincidence!" Yes, that's right. A God-planned coincidence. Step-by-step leading where needed details fall into perfect place because God planned them that way.

Closed doors may offer even clearer direction. Paul tells us that the Holy Spirit forbade him from speaking the word in Asia. Nor did the Spirit of Jesus allow him and Timothy to go into Bithynia (Acts 16:6-7). Yet that apparent failure became eventual success when Paul began missionary work in Europe.

When the Lord started directing us toward moving to northwest Wisconsin, we put our Minnesota house up for sale. I cleaned and cleaned and cleaned. I did everything humanly possible to make our home attractive. Finally one of my friends said,

"Lois, no matter how much you clean, your house isn't going to sell unless God wants it to."

The lack of sale was a closed door. Two years later, when it was God's timing for us to move, he opened the door. Three buyers fought over who would get our hard-to-sell house!

Words and Actions of Others

Paul knew the danger of going to Jerusalem yet felt compelled by the Spirit to go (Acts 20:22-23). Later the prophet Agabus took Paul's belt, used it to tie his own hands and feet, and confirmed what Paul already sensed: "The Holy Spirit says, 'In this way the Jews of Jerusalem will bind the owner of this belt and will hand him over to the Gentiles'" (Acts 21:10-14 NIV). Paul was being prepared for his victorious testimony as a prisoner.

If it's important that we know something, God often speaks in more than one way. Using different sources or people unknown to one another, the Holy Spirit verifies his leading by giving almost exactly the same message to more than one person.

Within two weeks after the diagnosis of cancer, I received mail from all parts of the United States. Within three weeks cards came from other countries. The notes that meant the most to me were ones on which people had written a verse. Some passages, such as Psalm 30 and Isaiah 41:10, were offered more than once. Scriptures not frequently used in connection with illness particularly interested me.

Soon I noticed a definite pattern. From people spread far apart geographically came a common message of encouragement. None of these people knew I was asking, "Lord, am I going to live, or do you want me to get ready to die?" Certainly it wouldn't be hard to guess I might be asking that question. But the overall effect of receiving a certain kind of verse helped me believe that God wanted me to pray for healing.

In those weeks following surgery my telephone rang often. Two messages offered special inspiration to my faith. "Lois, I don't know if you remember me," a caller began, "but you spoke at our church last fall. In February the Spirit woke me up one night, telling me to pray for you. He kept reminding me to continue, but I didn't understand why until today."

She paused, then went on. "Goose bumps went down my arms when your name came through our prayer chain. It was the first I heard about you having cancer."

The warm sense of being cared for as a child of God flooded my being. Others had told me that countless individuals who knew my situation were praying. But here was something different. It seemed the Lord also wanted those who hadn't heard in a natural way to be interceding. Moreover, the Holy Spirit had prompted this woman to pray even before my April 4 surgery.

Within four days a second call revealed a similar experience. Leah lived 170 miles from me and did not know the woman who had called. "Lois, I'm curious to know the date of your mastectomy," she began. "In the first part of April God started urging me to pray for you. The reminders were so insistent that it bothered me. When I came to Minneapolis for a meeting, I asked the other women, 'Does anyone know anything about Lois Johnson?' A neighbor of yours was there and answered, 'Yes.'"

These instances were encouragement situations, not directive ones. If God truly speaks through people, their words will be consistent with the basic teachings of Scripture.

As I faced cancer, a number of people said, "The Lord told me I should tell you this. . . ." In all but a few instances my inner spirit responded positively to their messages. On a rare occasion when I wondered if I should believe a person's words, I followed a checkpoint: *If God wants you to know something, he usually reveals it to you first, then uses other persons or situations to confirm your leading.*

Because persons say to me, "The Lord told me this," that does not mean I should accept their revelations without using the intellect, discernment, and common sense God gave me. In dealing with advice or encouragement offered by others, I need to experience a corresponding certainty. The verses given to me by friends usually echoed passages the Holy Spirit had illuminated in my daily Bible reading.

If uneasy about revelations from others, I guard against directive advice. In 1 Thessalonians 5:19-21, Paul tells us, "Do not quench the Spirit, do not despise prophesying, but test everything." It is not a lack of faith to ask God to confirm whether a message is truly of him.

Scripture promises us the ability to sift out truth from the misrepresentation or confusion of Satan. That discernment is possible only if we keep our focus on Christ and immerse ourselves in prayer and the daily study of Scripture. I'm most trustful of the answer coming through other people if I have prayed about a situation and God responds through people unaware of my concern.

God's Provision

Through confirming circumstances and provision, God gives both a promise and a checkpoint: *If God wants you to do something, there will be a way to do it.* As Hudson Taylor said, "Depend upon it, God's work, done in God's way, will never lack God's supplies."

Sometimes money arrives in one lump sum, the correct amount to the penny. On other occasions it comes a bit here, a bit there, as though God wants to test my faith. Occasionally I've been grateful that there hasn't been the money for what I wanted to do. I would have run ahead of God's plan.

Testing the Waters

If you are praying about something crucial and still feel doubtful about what to do, you may need to wait for a time. In lifelong choices, such as whether to marry a person, it could be disastrous if you moved ahead while still uncertain about what God wants.

With such a crucial decision as entering into a marriage, you must *know* that you *know* that you *know*.

On other occasions, however, you may believe you've heard the Lord, but aren't quite certain. God may be waiting for you to act on what you know before he shows you the next step.

A university career counselor told me that many young people are afraid to decide on a career in case they might be wrong. They waste an enormous amount of time and energy because they believe their decision is so important that they're afraid to make it. He tells the students, "Declare your concentration. Take classes in it. As you do, you'll test out whether you've made the right choice."

When we are Christians, God gives us that same opportunity. If you've done your best to discover his will, act on what you believe. When the children of Israel needed to cross the Jordan, God didn't part the waters until the priests at the head of the procession stretched out their feet to take the first step (Josh. 3:13-17). God blesses our being in motion. If you truly have heard him, he'll part the waters.

If, on the other hand, you have honestly sought him but haven't heard correctly, he'll protect you. He will block the way and bring a correction in your spirit, *providing you stay open to him.* If you have that sense of restraint in your spirit, stop what you're doing and seek the Lord again.

When Christ spoke to the two men on the road to Emmaus, they did not recognize him. Afterwards, when their eyes and spirits were opened, they acknowledged the truth of his words by saying, "Did not our hearts burn within us while he talked to us on the road, while he opened to us the scriptures?" (Luke 24:32).

In whatever you face, confusing circumstances give you the opportunity to trust in our Shepherd's gracious leading. If your spiritual pores are open to his direction, the Holy Spirit will strip away confusion, take what is true, and bless you with an undivided heart.

FAITH THOUGHT

TEACH ME YOUR WAY, O LORD, AND I WILL WALK IN YOUR
TRUTH; GIVE ME AN UNDIVIDED HEART, THAT I MAY FEAR
YOUR NAME. (PS. 86:11 NIV)

Sometimes I'm confused, Lord,
even shaky on the inside
when I hear of wars,
rumors of war,
economic disasters,
or catastrophic weather.
Other times I'm deeply concerned
about what's happening
to my loved ones or me.
Remind me, Lord,
that confusion and fear limit me
and your faith strengthens.
Help me to hear you so well
that even in uncertain times
I am certain of what
you want me to know.
Give me an undivided heart
that recognizes your voice,
then follows you.

GOD'S PROVISION FOR WHOLENESS

I believe I have a big God,
and I really need him now.
How can I ask him
for physical healing?

ABOUT A YEAR BEFORE I was diagnosed with cancer, I became deeply interested in the verses about biblical healing. As I taught those truths, I led people in praying for physical healing. Then suddenly I faced a life-threatening diagnosis of cancer. *How embarrassing!* I thought, when I had time to get past the initial dread. *What if I die at the age of forty? What are all those people going to think?*

It wasn't long before I realized that if I was headed for the grave, embarrassment really didn't count. I also recalled that I wasn't the one in charge of my healing. While I could cooperate with the Lord and ask for healing on this earth, whether I lived or died was ultimately up to him. As I reached that happy thought, the Lord gave me another—*Either way, I win.* No one could argue with that.

Now it was my turn to ask, "What kind of healing will be mine?" If I died, I would know soon enough. If I lived, it might take years to know, and who, if any of us, has a guarantee on the length of our lives.

To those who wondered, *If you had prayer before surgery, why didn't God heal you without a mastectomy?* I could only say, "He *did* heal me spiritually and emotionally. I feel more than compensated for what I've lost by the understanding I've gained."

As we pray for physical health, it's important to understand the close connection with our spiritual, emotional, and intellectual well-being. What does it mean to be led by a God so big that he cares about even the smallest detail of what happens to one of his own?

It's easy to be skeptical about praying for physical health if one has no need. Some people feel reluctant to pray because they don't understand that spiritual healing ministers to the whole person. In *Healing: A Spiritual Adventure,* Mary Peterman explains her belief in the love of God that is divine healing. Healing prayer seeks the wellness of the entire person: "If you believe that Christ is raised from the dead, that he forgives and loves and blesses, can you not also believe that he heals in body, mind, and spirit?"

When people came to Christ, asking for healing, at no time did he say, "Just a minute. I have to check with the Father to see if it's his will to heal you." Instead Jesus regarded illness of any kind as his enemy. In love and authority he simply reached out his hand in love and gave wholeness.

After returning home from the hospital, I reread the gospel of Luke because tradition says the author was a doctor. I felt especially struck by the instructions of Jesus in Luke 9: "And he called the twelve together and gave them power and authority over all demons and to cure diseases, and he sent them out to preach the kingdom of God and to heal" (vv. 1-2). A little conjunction, the three-letter word *and*, connects preaching the kingdom and healing the sick.

Luke describes what happened to the disciples: "And they departed and went through the villages, preaching the gospel and healing everywhere" (v. 6). In the early Christian church, the one followed the other as night follows day—preaching the good news, then healing. For the disciples Christianity had a practical application.

Throughout the Gospels, a variety of healings in the name of Jesus underscore his words. Gifts of healing were also given to the disciples as confirmation of their message. In Mark 16:16-18 Christ appears to the eleven, tells them to preach the gospel, and offers a promise with no time limitation:

> *And these signs will accompany those who believe: in my name they will cast out demons; they will speak in new tongues; they will pick up serpents, and if they drink any deadly thing, it will not hurt them; they will lay their hands on the sick; and they will recover.*

Clearly Jesus expected those who preached the gospel to perform signs in his name. Whether we pray for others or ourselves, there's a life principle involved:

> *When we seek Jesus for*
> *healing of body, mind, and*
> *spirit, he reaches out to touch*
> *us at our point of need.*

As I considered the number of promises given in connection with healing, I asked several questions about which you might also wonder:

1) How can I pray more effectively for divine healing?

When Jesus healed people, he touched them. Therefore, if a person is comfortable with it, I pray in the same way. I simply put my hands on the head or shoulders of the person needing wholeness. Through the sense of touch and in answer to prayer, Christ's power and love flow through me into the individuals for whom I pray.

For years J. Reed's painting of Christ's outstretched hands hung in my kitchen where I could see it whenever I glanced up from preparing a meal. "Come unto Me," the painting quietly reminds. When Jesus told his disciples how to enter a town, he said, "Heal the sick in it and say to them, 'The kingdom of God has come near to you'" (Luke 10:9). When I pray for wholeness for someone, I believe I am going in Jesus' name and obeying his promise: "He who believes in me will also do the works that I do; and greater works than these will he do, because I go to the Father" (John 14:12).

In seeking divine healing for others, I request guidance, either silently or aloud, and ask that the Spirit give his words and wisdom. With each circumstance the actual words of prayer vary, but certain basics are helpful.

First, because Christ described illness as the bondage of Satan (Luke 13:16), I pray, "In the name of Jesus I bind the power of Satan." Next I request wholeness, again using the name of Jesus: "In the strong name of Jesus I ask for healing from _____ [name the illness and whatever specific needs exist]." Then I thank God immediately, as instructed in Philippians 4:6.

A person confronted by a serious illness may ask for the power of united prayer. Practices vary. Some churches use prepared liturgical services. With others the service is informal. Five and a half months after surgery I found another lump, and family and friends gathered for a prayer service in our chapel.

After sharing meaningful Scripture verses, we participated in Holy Communion. Then the pastor prayed, "Lord, stir up the gifts of healing," and put a small amount of oil on my forehead, anointing me with the sign of the cross in the name of the Father, Son, and Holy Spirit. Those around me placed their hands on my shoulders or head and prayed in faith for my healing.

When my friends and family finished, I also prayed, thanking God in faith for his healing. Others joined in giving thanks, and we sang praise songs, for the Lord dwells in the praises of his people.

Such services follow the instructions given by James:

Is any among you sick? Let him call for the elders of the church, and let them pray over him, anointing him with oil in the name of the Lord; and the prayer of faith will save the sick man, and the Lord will raise him up; and if he has committed sins, he will be forgiven. (James 5:14-15)

As a cancer patient, I took seriously my need to search my heart about any sin I had committed and ask forgiveness before others began praying. If I am bottling up resentment or bitterness, I also need to get rid of that by forgiving whoever might be involved (see chapters 8 and 9). Often a pastor gives time at the beginning of a healing service for everyone to silently ask forgiveness for sin. It's important to not let any blockage hinder our prayers (Ps. 66:18).

By following the instructions in James, each local congregation is not only being scriptural but also has the resources to minister to the practical and spiritual needs of its people. The anointing of oil has both spiritual and physical significance.

The Bible shows oil as one of the symbols of the Holy Spirit. In his book *A Shepherd Looks at Psalm 23*, Philip Keller gives an additional understanding to the words "He anoints my head with oil." Summertime flies pestered the shepherd's flock, torturing his sheep and driving them almost to distraction. Trying to escape their tormentors, some of the sheep became frantic with fear and raced around the pasture, hoping to elude the flies. The moment the shepherd applied oil to the heads of his sheep, their behavior changed immediately.

What can that anointing of oil mean for us? Just as sheep need an ongoing application of oil, so do we need the continuous anointing of God's Spirit in order to live our daily lives and walk in his power and wholeness. When we combine the anointing of oil with prayer, we invite the healing presence of Jesus. We also pray as taught in the book of James.

Those who feel reluctant to ask others to pray in this way demonstrate a misunderstanding of God's goodness. As one pastor said, "When people become ill, they often say, 'Will you pray for me?' But often they're afraid to ask, 'Will you pray *for healing* for me?'" Patients who do not receive the anointing of the church miss out on promised power, and fail to experience the love felt in such services. That love is another form of healing.

I believe every right prayer is answered, that every person who asks receives some form of healing. But it's important to pray in an atmosphere of love, not guaranteeing which kind of healing—emotional, spiritual, physical, or intellectual—will come to a person. While Christ commands and expects his people to pray, he has the overall perspective and makes the decision about how the answer comes.

2) How are prayers for physical wholeness answered?
Sometimes people miss seeing God at work because they think prayers should be answered instantaneously. The Bible shows several ways in which answers came:

> *Immediate healing:* Notice the natural outcome. The woman praised God (Luke 13:10-13).
> *Gradual healing:* Christ used spit (medication and surgery?) and prayed more than once (Mark 8:22-25).
> *After a delay:* sometimes emotional and spiritual blocks must be dealt with before physical healing takes place (Luke 17:11-19).
> *Healing in connection with the forgiveness of sins:* (John 5:2-16).
> *After an inward revelation of God:* God showed himself to Job (Job 42:5).
> *Ultimate or perfect healing:* Eternal life because the person prayed for is spiritually whole. He or she asked forgiveness for sin and received the salvation Jesus offers through his death on the cross (John 11:25-26).

All of these kinds of healing occur in the present day.

3) What is spiritual and emotional wholeness?
Always I try to be conscious of the interrelatedness of spirit, soul, and body. When I pray for others, I ask the Spirit to make me aware if there are spiritual or emotional blockages that would interfere with physical healing. If there is time to intercede adequately, I seldom pray for someone's physical wholeness without seeing the need to ask for the spiritual and emotional.

My friend, Pat Rosenberg, who lived daily with a child severely handicapped by cerebral palsy, often prayed, "Lord, help me to be content with who I am and in spite of the circumstances confronting me." That's spiritual and emotional wholeness.

Paul expressed a similar view: "I have learned, in whatever state I am, to be content" (Phil. 4:11). Often I am aware that the most important healing is spiritual. The next is emotional, for spiritual and emotional strength sustain me when physical health is absent.

Our greatest wholeness is salvation and the eternal life it gives. There is also a wholeness of spirit that comes when we face extremely difficult circumstances and know that Jesus is Lord in spite of all that has happened. In his suffering Job experienced an inward revelation: "Then I knew only what others had told me, but now I have seen you with my own eyes" (Job 42:5 TEV). After he prayed for his friends, God made Job prosperous again, blessing the last part of his life even more than the first.

Over twenty-three years ago, while still on chemotherapy, I wrote: "Because of all I have learned through the prayer relationship, I believe the segment of my life since my mastectomy has been more blessed than the first. I have lived the meaning of the words, 'Look to the Giver, not to the gift.' As I continue to pray for wholeness, I focus my thoughts on that Giver—not having faith in faith, but faith in the Lord Jesus Christ. I ask for healing with one underlying thought: that in my search for wholeness I see Christ with my own eyes. For then whichever way the ultimate answer comes, I am held in his arms, knowing his love, knowing that either way, I win."

FAITH THOUGHT

SHE HAD HEARD THE REPORTS ABOUT JESUS, AND CAME UP BEHIND HIM IN THE CROWD AND TOUCHED HIS GARMENT. FOR SHE SAID, "IF I TOUCH EVEN HIS GARMENTS, I SHALL BE MADE WELL." AND IMMEDIATELY THE HEMORRHAGE

CEASED; AND SHE FELT IN HER BODY THAT SHE WAS HEALED
OF HER DISEASE. . . . [JESUS] SAID TO HER, "DAUGHTER,
YOUR FAITH HAS MADE YOU WELL; GO IN PEACE, AND BE
HEALED OF YOUR DISEASE." (MARK 5:27-29, 34)

> Jesus,
> whenever I feel
> that physical wholeness
> is an impossibility,
> remind me that you
> are the one
> who changes lives.
> Remind me of that woman
> who simply reached out,
> believed in you,
> then knew
> that you had healed her.
>
> Jesus, you turned to her.
> You said that powerful word I need:
> "Daughter, your faith
> has made you well.
> Be freed from your suffering!"
>
> Lord Jesus,
> Help me to simply reach up,
> to touch your robe in faith.
> In your name I ask
> that you heal me of my trouble,
> that you speak your word of power.
> In faith I thank you!
> I praise you, Lord!
> I go in peace.

CHAPTER THIRTEEN

MAKING CHRISTIANITY PRACTICAL

———◆●◆———

Walk in faith?
Keep a healing?
What do you mean?
How can I know more
about the variety of ways
in which the Lord works?

SHORTLY AFTER DOCTORS TOLD ME I HAD CANCER, I discovered two kinds of people. There were those who were comfortable about being with me even though I had received a life-threatening diagnosis. And there were those who were not.

Frequently the individuals who fell into the comfortable category believed in praying for healing. I needed to be with them, because they encouraged my faith. One of these was Dave, a young man of twenty-two. When he heard my situation, he said, "I'll tell other people about you. We'll all pray."

Soon I learned that many of the people I had taught to pray over the years had begun praying for me. Often I felt their intercessions through peace and the sense of being loved. That spiritual and emotional support answered the question individuals sometimes ask, "What if we pray for people and they aren't healed? Won't they lose their faith?"

I felt just the opposite—grateful for strength-giving prayer and for anyone who was not afraid to pray against cancer. I thought, *Even if their prayers aren't answered on this earth, at least they're trying.*

In contrast to those who were afraid to pray, the people who prayed in love were easier to live with. They provided a loving community, an emotional and spiritual support group. They knew what to do with me and simply brought each new need to God. That was their way of making Christianity practical.

As we pray for physical health, it's important to understand the close connection with our spiritual, emotional, and intellectual well-being. When Jesus described himself as the door of the sheep, he understood that need: "I am the door; if anyone enters by me, he will be saved, and will go in and out and find pasture" (John 10:9).

Jesus is the door by which we enter into salvation. There is no other way for us to enter into eternal life. As the Good Shepherd, Jesus also protects the access by which his sheep go in and out of the sheepfold. What does it mean to live in a sheepfold that offers the life and healing we need? What, after all, *is* a sheepfold?

In his book *A Shepherd Looks at the Good Shepherd and His Sheep,* Phillip Keller describes it for us. The walls of the sheepfold may be made of rough-laid stones, sun-dried bricks, timber, mud and wattle, or even tightly packed thorn brush. From country to country, the materials used in the wall change, but the sheepfold always has one purpose—to provide protection.

Yet this shelter is not something tight and confining. The sheepfold is not a barn, shed, closed-in or roofed-over structure but is open to the wind, sun, and rain. The sheep live under the stars, moon, and sky. While knowing the watchful eye of their shepherd, they also enjoy the sense of being outdoors.

When Jesus offers his sheltering presence, he gives us that same freedom. Though we come to him for physical health, we receive much more. As we stand in the freedom of his presence, he responds in a variety of ways. What are some questions that will help us see his answers?

1) How important is the faith of the patient?

It's possible to block healing by refusing to believe that Christ acts on our behalf. Matthew tells us, "And he did not do many mighty works there, because of their unbelief" (Matt. 13:58). Faith on the part of someone is necessary.

I'm always afraid for people who have the opportunity for someone to pray for them, yet turn it down because they think, *I might be uncomfortable with that. or I don't know if I want to be anointed with oil. I mean, that's kind of strange, isn't it?*

To me it's much more uncomfortable to die prematurely than to be anointed with oil. I felt grateful for anyone who made the effort to pray, either beside me or from a distance. I also jumped at every opportunity in which people were willing to anoint me with oil. Just as Phillip Keller's sheep needed many applications of oil, so do I benefit from being anointed with oil more than once—or as often as seems appropriate.

When praying for others, I feel most hopeful of good results when a sick person has a cooperative, expectant, faith-filled attitude. The healing passage in James reminds us that it's important for a patient to deal with any known sin or other blockage, such as needing to forgive someone. A patient needs to seek the Lord and immerse himself or herself in Scripture. But someone who is ill should not feel responsible for bringing all the faith needed for a difficult healing. That's where the body of Christ becomes important.

Misunderstanding of this puts an added burden upon a patient and also creates problems in those who are not healed physically. Some of us interceded for Martha Cameron, a lovely friend we called "Grandma." Years before the Salk vaccine, one of her sons contracted polio at the age of two. For a time everyone wondered if Bruce would live, let alone walk again, but Grandma prayed in faith. One morning hospital nurses found Bruce standing up in his crib. Today he walks, serving as a medical doctor.

Knowing that part of Grandma Cameron's history encouraged me in asking for her healing. At first, as many prayed for her, Grandma's health improved. Then she reached a plateau. With tears in her eyes she said, "Lois, some people told me I would be healed if I had more faith. Is that what's wrong? That I don't have enough faith?"

Listening to her I felt as if a sword had pierced my heart. First, because of the insensitivity of people who had spoken in this way to a woman of God. But then I hurt even more because I believed it was her time to die.

I felt unsure about how to handle that kind of insight. Though I knew Grandma was eager to go home, I also knew that I might not be hearing correctly from the Lord. And so I answered, "Do you remember the different ways people were healed in the New Testament? The woman with a flow of blood was healed because of her own faith. But many others became well through the faith of the disciples or another person who came to Jesus and asked."

I cannot say strongly enough that members of the body of Christ share the responsibility to pray for one another. I quickly discovered that if I was discouraged or physically weak, I found it difficult to pray effectively for myself.

If I experienced an improvement or healing after the intercessions of others, I felt a responsibility to thank the people who prayed. I wanted to encourage their faith and join together in praising the Lord. As a friend said, "Persons may become whole because of the faith of someone else, but it's important that individuals who are healed praise God themselves, acknowledging their good health."

In cases where a healing cannot be medically proven except through time, persons who sense they have been spiritually healed should continue to thank the Lord for it. These patients will also benefit by telling only the right people—ones who believe in Christ's healing power—so they do not become discouraged by continually meeting unbelief.

After my conversation with Grandma Cameron, I began to pray in a different way: "Lord, I ask for your perfect healing for Grandma." I wanted to give God the opportunity to act in the best way possible. If my inward sense was right, she would be allowed to go home, as she wanted. If I was wrong in what I sensed, my prayers would contribute to her health on this earth. Only a few months later she quietly slipped home, and I imagined her saying, "Praise the Lord!"

2) What about the medical profession and divine healing?

For me it's important to take advantage of all God's resources. When I need physical healing, God wants me to value the knowledge and abilities of medical people. As a Christian facing cancer, I felt it was important to support the skill of my doctors with prayer.

While lying on the surgical table, one of our friends asked his surgeon, "Do you mind if I pray for you before we start?" The surgeon looked startled, then said, "I'd like that. I've never had a patient offer to pray with me before."

In the best situation, praying Christians and the medical profession combine resources. When prayer supplements the practice of medicine, it may help the natural healing process.

At times I've noticed an unusual pattern after prayers for physical healing. A close friend described it this way: "When my dad received a diagnosis of cancer of the kidney, a nurse looked at me and shook her head. She knew that cancer might already have spread throughout his body. Yet when we prayed in agreement as a family, I felt led to pray, 'Lord Jesus, in your name, we ask you to simply cast the cancer out of Dad's body.' I truly did not know what I was saying.

"After surgery the doctor told us, 'I found that all the cancer was encapsulated in one kidney. I removed that kidney, and your dad will be just fine. He won't even need to have chemotherapy.'"

Aha! The surgeon literally cast the kidney out! My friend could have said, "That was certainly a coincidence," and talked herself out of belief in God's healing power. Instead she thanked him for his answer to prayer.

In common with others who pray for healing, I've often encountered something that can't be explained. For instance, a doctor runs a number of tests and makes a diagnosis, possibly a very disheartening one. The patient asks his pastor, priest, relatives, or friends for prayer. When a biopsy is done, the final report is not as bleak as the first expectation.

I believe that doctors have enough knowledge and scientific tests at their disposal that in most cases they make the right diagnoses. So what has happened between that original diagnosis and the biopsy? Prayers of faith on the part of God's people!

When good things happen, it is sometimes difficult to know what is the result of a medical procedure and what is a direct answer to prayer. When people try to decide between the two, I can only say, "Does it matter? God uses medicine. He uses medical people. He answers prayer. If a patient is doing well, just praise God!"

There's another life principle involved:

> *A faith that works in real*
> *life leads to a team effort for*
> *making Christianity practical.*

Because there are so many things that can go wrong during an illness, I don't worry about proof or defending God's honor. He can defend himself. But I *do* want to be sure that I'm thankful and acknowledge God's help, both in my private prayers and when I talk to others. Good results act as seed in the ground, contributing toward someone's belief. As one doctor said, "I have more reason than anyone to believe in divine healing. Things happen that I know go far beyond any skill or power I possess medically."

In recent years the medical community has confirmed what Christians have known all along. In an article for the Lutheran Brotherhood's magazine *Bond*, Bill Vossler wrote:

> *Draw on your faith. A growing number of medical studies show*
> *that people who have strong religious beliefs are likely to be*
> *healthier and live longer than those who are less religious. They*
> *have lower blood pressure and stronger immune systems, lower*
> *stress and recover more quickly from depression and serious surgery.*
> *Make prayer a lifestyle.*

After the circumstances of my illness became widely known, people I didn't know wrote to tell me I should have the faith to go off chemotherapy and claim my healing. When I first read such advice, it gave me unrest. By the time I received a number of letters with the same advice, I felt what I hope can be described as righteous indignation. In the months immediately after surgery, I was not receiving any indication from God that I was to go off chemotherapy. Instead I believed it was part of God's healing that I lived at a time when chemotherapy was available to me. It was frightening for me to think, *What if I were an immature Christian and felt the pressure of that advice without the Lord's leading?*

As a cancer patient, I was not alone in this problem. Others on long-term medication and those who suffer from chronic illness sometimes face the same advice. People who refuse to use doctors or medicine may be limiting God by insisting on the way they want their healing to come.

3) How can I pray against medicinal side effects for people?

In that time before the improved antinausea medicine we now have, I deeply valued any nurse who prayed with me against side effects as she gave me treatments. After being on chemotherapy for fifteen months, I found myself spiritually exhausted.

Certain friends were especially effective as intercessors. Often they called, saying, "How are you?" and I'd tell them. I hoped they would pray, but sometimes I was afraid to ask them again. Just the same, I knew when they did, because I began feeling better, either emotionally or physically, or both.

Sometimes patients think that if they've been prayed for once, they shouldn't ask for more prayer. Even as I need to eat three times a day, so do I need the emotional and spiritual sustenance God gives in answer to the prayers of his people. If patients have the freedom to ask for prayer, their frustrations and needs won't be as likely to build into an overwhelming mountain. In recent years e-mail has opened the way for united prayer in the name of Jesus. "I've become part of a group praying for a relative I've never met," said one man. "Each time he gives a report and tells us to thank the Lord, I feel the bond of a special gift. Together we're a team, praying for a loved one's healing."

If you belong to a praying family, meals or before-bed talk time can be the perfect place to give or receive prayer. Often I asked my husband and children to pray for me with laying on of hands—putting their hands on my back or shoulders. We trusted the promise of Jesus: "Where two or three are gathered in my name, there am I in the midst of them" (Matt. 18:20). We asked that God would make the medicine do what it was supposed to do but also protect me from side effects. More than once I felt better instantly.

During that time I repeatedly learned the importance of knowing Scripture. One day I came home after chemo injections and crawled into bed. I just wanted to sleep so I could forget how miserable I felt. I thought, *Maybe if I don't move my head even one inch, I won't throw up.*

In that moment the tiny whisper of the Spirit reminded me of a verse I had memorized: "If they drink any deadly thing, it will not hurt them . . ." (Mark 16:18).

With a rush of gratitude I prayed, "Thank you, Jesus. You have promised that even poison will not make your disciples sick!" Instantly my nausea vanished. I got up and made supper for my family. I even ate with them.

About the same time a friend said, "Tell us the days you have your injections. We'll send your name through our prayer chain each time." Though my drug dosage increased, I found those prayers made an incredible difference—much less nausea and of shorter duration. Of course, I also had to cooperate, taking time for needed rest.

Those confronted by serious illness know that the presence of hair is not the indicator of good health. Yet hair or a lack of it deeply influences morale. When I first went on chemo, I was on one drug and had too much pride to ask people to pray about my hair. *I can pray myself*, I thought.

I couldn't. In that time, most of us wore a wig instead of the attractive hats and scarves patients often use now. I lost so much hair I had to wear a hot, uncomfortable wig for five months. Friends of mine, Joyce and Leigh Wold, decided to pray and fast for a day. Soon after, my chemo dosage was lowered for a short time. My hair began coming back in and stayed, even when the dosage increased once more.

At that point I began seeing an oncologist who put me on a combination of three drugs. Again I started losing hair, and again Joyce and Leigh fasted for a day. In the months that followed, my hair thinned out but the rate of loss slowed down when they or other friends interceded for me. Even though I was taking more chemo than before, I did not have to return to wearing a wig.

Those familiar with chemotherapy know that drugs that kill cancer cells also destroy white blood cells. By keeping track of my hemoglobin and white blood counts, I discovered that both counts recovered more quickly when I had frequent prayer with laying on of hands or consistently took Holy Communion. At the time, we attended a church where we were able to take communion every Sunday after the last service. During that time Roy and I silently prayed in agreement, asking Jesus to give healing.

Because my hemoglobin and white blood counts bounced back, my oncologist was able to keep increasing my chemo dosage. When I didn't have the opportunity for communion or became careless in asking for prayer, both my hemoglobin and white blood counts remained low. My participation in communion and the prayers I received were measurable!

Members of a sacramental church should be aware of the power available when meeting Christ in Holy Communion. Often I kneel at the altar, not only in recommitment, confession, praise, and thanksgiving, but also in supplication—for myself and for the spiritual, emotional, or physical needs of others.

4) What if I feel unsure about how to pray?
When Christ was here on earth, he reached out and healed everyone who came to him. Therefore I pray for healing unless God shows me otherwise.

With a person who has been seriously ill for some time, I ask for guidance before praying. Sometimes I've received a nudge from the Spirit to ask in faith for good health. On other occasions I have sensed a quietness in my spirit or received a verse such as Hebrews 9:27 that led me to believe it was time for someone to die.

Often I ask a seriously ill person, "How do you want me to pray?" If that individual asks me to pray for healing, I believe the Spirit has inspired that faith. We pray in agreement about the kind of healing that is needed.

I've also learned to ask, "What kind of verses are you receiving from the Lord?" One spiritually mature woman answered, "The healing verses are nice, but my husband and I are receiving the comforting ones."

In *The Power to Heal* Francis MacNutt offers a suggestion made by a friend:

> She always prays "for healing," but not excluding death, a kind of ultimate healing. For the believer, eternal life has already begun; so bodily death is an event within eternal life. You can pray for the person's healing without necessarily praying against death. You can pray that the person be as whole as possible and ready for full union with Jesus, and leave it up to him what that might mean concretely. You can always pray for more of the life of God to enter into that person. And this just might be eternal life.

When unsure about how to pray, I also ask the Holy Spirit to pray through me. In Romans 8:26 Paul writes, "Likewise the Spirit helps us in our weakness; for we do not know how to pray as we ought, but the Spirit himself intercedes for us with signs too deep for words."

As I faced cancer, I did not ask the question, "Can Christ heal?" I knew he could. But I prayed, "Lord, is it my time to live or my time to die?" When offering that prayer I needed to accept the kind of leading given to me. I believed that if it were my time to die, the Spirit would illuminate passages that encouraged me to ask for strength, freedom from pain, and a happy homegoing. By contrast, in the time following surgery, the verses highlighted were clearly ones encouraging my faith to ask for physical healing. I knew that at some future time I might receive a different kind of leading.

Friendship or family groups offer an ideal place for the ongoing, persistent, soaking prayer needed with chronic illness. Often children have a greater faith and can pray more effectively than adults. If praying about someone seriously ill, however, it's important to explain the various ways healing comes, including death as a possibility. After we received word that the cancer in my brother-in-law Harv had spread, I said to our children, "Let's continue praying in faith for his healing. But let's understand that sometimes God answers with a perfect healing. He might allow Harv to go to heaven so he can have a new body—a perfect one that won't hurt anymore."

5) *What if my prayers for physical healing are not answered?*
Only two months before surgery, I had finished a chapter for my book *Gift in My Arms*. After explaining how to pray with the biblical laying on of hands, I said: "When we pray for physical healing, we realize there are circumstances in which the kingdom of God has not yet come perfectly on this earth. As Christians, we believe that ultimate healing comes in the resurrection. We don't need to lose our faith because of the way the answer to prayer comes. While we seek physical wholeness, we understand other kinds of healing can be even more important."

Those who have dealt with possible blockages and are not receiving physical wholeness might pray, "Lord, I give my situation to you, asking that you use it for good in the lives of others." Yet it is important to come to this only after praying in faith for healing. In the classic devotional *My Utmost for His Highest* Oswald Chambers writes:

> *Abraham did not choose what the sacrifice would be. Always guard against self-chosen service for God. Self-sacrifice may be a*

disease that impairs your service. If God has made your cup sweet, drink it with grace; or even if He has made it bitter, drink it in communion with Him. If the providential will of God means a hard and difficult time for you, go through it. But never decide the place of your own martyrdom.

I don't know if my brother-in-law Harv offered his cancer for good in the lives of others, but I believe his suffering was used in a redemptive manner. Before cancer, he was the kind of pastor who went into a small-town restaurant for coffee to become acquainted with people who were reluctant to come to church. During his long illness, staff from throughout the hospital came to his room to help him. With each of these people, as well as his visitors, he talked. After his death one nurse said, "We've seen many people die. But we've never seen anyone die the way Harvey Johnson did."

A man and his wife asked me, "Lois, what should we do? I've had many years beyond the time doctors thought I would live. Now I'm slipping again. I have to decide if I'm willing to take more chemotherapy, even if it falls into the experimental category."

He looked at his wife with a sad, gentle smile. "I have to decide whether I'm willing to fight again. Fight to live, I mean. But what if it's my time to die? If it is, I don't want to waste whatever time I have left in trying things that aren't going to work. I want to spend whatever time I have talking with my loved ones."

Those are hard decisions. I respected that man because he was facing things honestly and openly. We decided to pray that he and his wife would be agreed in hearing what God wanted.

It's important to remember a balance between prayers of faith and relinquishment. One patient told me, "If it's my time to die, I want to go home rather than suffer." She was receiving strengthening, rather than healing, passages. A short time after group prayer in which she, her relatives, and friends put the situation into God's hands, the woman died without experiencing the pain or problems she feared.

If God reveals it's time to die, those surrounding a patient have the responsibility of relinquishment. I've heard Christians say, "Let's pray for a happy death for my loved one." Always the answer came in a beautiful homegoing.

When my husband's first wife, Connie, had suffered for some time, he reached the point of praying, "Lord, I give her to you." My sister-in-law Betty uttered almost the same words when her husband Harv was dying of cancer: "Lord, I turn him over to you." Often it's the person closest to a patient who needs to relinquish the loved one. Anguishing as the prayer is, that also is making Christianity practical. Both Connie and Harv died within a few days after being given to God.

6) What if I believe I've been healed but can't prove it?

Persons who believe they have received physical healing have both an opportunity and a responsibility to act wisely.

Remember the words of my surgeon? "You'll be on chemotherapy the rest of your life." Remember, too, the many advances in diagnosis and treatment options since then. In common with everyone who knew me, I wondered how long my life would be. But whether short or long, I felt destined to be on chemotherapy. Then after many months—fifteen or so—I began to grow restless. I asked God to show me what I needed to know. I prayed, "Lord, if it's safe for me to go off chemo, will you tell me through my doctor?"

After praying at least a month about it, I asked my oncologist. He said, "Well, let's wait until—" I can't remember the reason he gave, but it was very specific and reasonable. He had in mind a definite goal involving a certain number of treatments.

I accepted his decision. I still felt restless, but I believed that God would use my specialist to show me what I needed to do.

About two months later, I asked a women's prayer group to pray about the situation. Still planning to do whatever my oncologist said, I returned for my next appointment. I didn't ask him again about going off chemo, but that day he looked back through my chart. After reviewing my medical history since surgery, he looked up and said, "I believe it's safe for you to go off chemotherapy."

You might find it interesting that this particular doctor had told me he wasn't a Christian. If God wants you released from chemotherapy, it's no problem for him to speak to your doctor, whether he or she is a believer or not. Your doctor will know if it's wise for you to go off medication.

With a great sense of relief I went off chemo. Does that mean that I always felt at peace about it? For the most part I did, but sometimes fear returned. I soon discovered that even though I had followed what I believed was God's leading, chemo had become an emotional crutch for me. Over the months it had started to represent safety. So far it had worked. Had I truly heard the Lord by stopping something that was "safe"?

During moments of questioning, I felt especially glad that I had waited for my doctor's release instead of insisting upon my own wishes. When attacked by fear, I needed to seek the Lord again. Each time I did he reassured me that the decision made through my doctor was the right one.

7) What does it mean to "stand in faith" for a healing?

Those familiar with the ministry of healing may hear someone say, "She lost her healing." When praying for others or ourselves, it's essential to understand an important concept. While we do not want to live in fear, we do need to stand in the place of victory God has given us.

After a person receives a verifiable healing, there may come a time of testing. It's as though Satan wants to tear away any glory that God might receive through his sovereign work. If such a testing comes, it's essential to stand on the Scripture that the Holy Spirit gives in connection with that healing. It's also necessary to stand in the name of Jesus, not denying reality, but in the healing he has already given. Pray in faith, thanking and praising the Lord for that healing.

Ten years before my mastectomy, my doctor told me I had rheumatoid arthritis. For seven years I experienced that pain and gnawing ache. For two of those years I ran a low-grade temperature. Each time I led an all-day prayer seminar, I found it

more difficult to stand because of pain in my knees. Finally I came
to a season in which I had promised to give seven seminars in a
short period of time. I looked ahead and thought only of the
agony of standing all day.

I knew I could not continue accepting invitations to speak,
but my need was immediate. How could I get through what I had
already promised? *I'm teaching people to pray,* I thought. *If God calls
me to do something, shouldn't I be able to do it?*

My health forced me to face something else. I had gotten into
the habit of keeping God in compartments. It was okay to have
him in one part of my life. But there were other areas in which I
wanted to do things my own way. Finally I knew that I needed to
stop boxing God in. I needed to surrender my will and allow him
to work in *every* area of my life. When I did that, I came to know
the Lord in a deeper way.

At first I didn't realize I had also experienced a spontaneous
remission from arthritis. The next day later I conducted an all-day
prayer seminar, and after standing nearly seven hours went home
feeling rested. Soon after, it snowed. For the first time in years I
hadn't received a warning when the weather system reached the
North Dakota border, heading our way.

Then the weather warmed, and one night I woke to the
sound of rain. Realizing it was the first time in seven years I had
been surprised by rain, I began thanking God.

Finally, after a month of good health, I told my husband and
two friends, "I believe I've had a remission from arthritis." I was
afraid to tell them what had happened, afraid that if I said I
was healed, my good health would disappear.

It did. Two mornings later I woke to the worst pain I had
experienced in some time. Every vertebrae and joint in my body
ached. All day I went around thinking, *I really didn't have a remission. I'll have to tell my husband I was wrong. Nothing happened.*

That night I slipped into bed, ready to fall apart from the
gnawing ache and the emotional letdown. Yet before falling
asleep, I sensed a quiet inner voice saying, *Lois, the first time I*

gave you your health as a free gift. Now I want you to have the faith to ask.

I did. "In the name of Jesus I ask for healing for my elbows, my fingers, my ankles, my knees, my vertebrae," I prayed. "Thank you, Jesus." In each place for which I prayed I felt heat.

Now, get up and walk, said the inward voice.

In the darkness of night I got up and walked around the house. And I didn't hurt anymore.

Did God's healing last? In the two and a half years immediately after this sovereign work, I again experienced testing. On three or four occasions, symptoms returned, making me anxious. I needed to pray with my will, "Lord Jesus, I believe Satan is trying to make me think nothing happened. In the name of Jesus, I believe you have made me whole. Thank you." Each time the symptoms disappeared.

In Luke 7:35 TEV Jesus said, "God's wisdom . . . is shown to be true by all who accept it." Those who have prayed in faith and have not been healed can offer their illness to God, saying, "Lord, use it for your kingdom." But if God gives you a healing, face whatever testing you might experience in the power of his name. Stand with the Lord to continue the healing that frees you to serve.

"Get up and walk, Lois. Get up and walk."

Faith Thought

"For I will restore health to you, and your wounds I will heal," says the Lord. (Jer. 30:17a)

Sometimes my life
seems like withered grass.
Yet, Lord, you hold out
the shelter of your sheepfold.
With your caring gaze you look on.
With your waiting presence
you protect the door,
encouraging me to go in and out
and seek green pasture.

I need that enclosure of your love,
the freedom of your open sky—
the stars and moon by night,
the rising sun by morning,
the rain of your cleansing,
and the wind of your new life.
Watch over me, Lord,
bring me to the pasture
of your healing.
Bring me to you!

HEALING FROM THE INSIDE OUT

———◆●◆———

Never perfect before,
less than perfect now,
how can I receive
the emotional healing I need?

W HEN I MET A DARK-EYED, ATTRACTIVE YOUNG WOMAN for lunch, she posed a question many had been afraid to ask: "How did you deal with the scar from your mastectomy?" I can't remember my exact response, but it was immediate and from the heart. To me the world is a place full of scars—reminders of lives that have been changed.

In the years since my surgery, our world has experienced countless medical and social changes. When diagnosed with breast cancer, women have a choice of more procedures and a greater involvement in the kind of treatment they prefer. In the time of my mastectomy, when reconstruction surgery was delayed or less often chosen by a woman, the question about a scar was an even greater concern. Today it remains crucial for every person who feels his or her body is less than perfect. Doesn't that include most, of not all, if us?

As I thought about it, I realized the potential power of any wound—physical, emotional, intellectual, or spiritual. If unhealed, an injury permanently affects self-esteem. If, instead, a wound heals from the inside out, there may be a mark, but the scar indicates progress. The individual has grown.

How might the choice of healing be ours?

Being a Woman

Something that has hurt us deeply can heal in an instant, but more often it involves a gradual process. Leaving injuries behind requires time alone in which we face and work through the situations causing hurt.

After my mastectomy, my doctor encouraged the use of my arm. Each morning during my hospital stay, I got up before my visitors arrived so I could wash my hair. I knew exactly what I was doing— compensating however I could. And though it might sound ridiculous to others that I washed my hair four times in four days, it helped me.

During my first bath, my incision was still an angry red line. The nurse left the room, and I was glad, for I needed to be alone to face what had happened. In that moment I knew that many friends were praying, for I sensed the supportive love of the Holy Spirit. I pushed back tears, thinking, *If it isn't worse than this, I can make it.*

Yet as I talked with a close friend, I was honest about how I felt. "It means so much to me to be a woman." The response was immediate: "Then be more of a woman in other ways."

I remembered those words often. As I dealt with all that had happened, many people contributed to my healing. The most important of these was my husband. Before surgery I warned Roy that I would probably have a mastectomy, but he did not believe me. After losing his first wife through illness, he was not able to take in my words.

One night when I was still in the hospital, Roy woke up crying. He wept until his pillow was wet with tears. In that time of new grief it seemed to him that there had been only a day between the death of his first wife and the reality that I, too, might die. But there was also something more.

"I know how important a breast is for a woman," he told me. "I wish I could wear that scar for you." Later he said, "When we were married the two of us became one flesh. That means your scar is my scar."

Roy's words reflected another life principle:

> *Pain understood by those who hold it*
> *with gentle hands becomes a precious bond.*

Dealing with Loss

For many women the terror of how they may look holds yet another fear: *Will my husband be unfaithful to me?* I can answer, "If your husband was that kind of person before your mastectomy, he may be again. If you had a good marital relationship before, it can continue. If your husband has been faithful to you, your mastectomy can draw you even closer." But if a mastectomy or any form of cancer is going to draw you closer, there are certain conditions that have to be met.

Too often I hear of marriages in jeopardy because a series of crises have destroyed communication between husband and wife. Those with serious bodily changes need to know that if there is a problem, it should not be blamed only on the surgery, in spite of what many people believe. The root of the question comes in whether *both* husband and wife are willing to face a situation and talk about it honestly. Both of them need to crash through any barriers that resist communication.

With any crisis or life-changing illness, the problem itself may not be as important as how we deal with it. One woman told me, "The first time I looked in a mirror without crying, I knew I had it licked. I think if we handle a mastectomy okay, our husbands do." She realized it is not a question of either-or. In every difficulty both husband and wife need to cope together, coming to acceptance.

At one point Roy told me, "I love you even more because you've been through something difficult." Since then I've learned of other husbands saying something similar to their wives. Yet some women respond as did one wife: "I couldn't believe he was telling the truth. I was the one who wouldn't accept the way I looked. That's what caused our marital problems."

From the beginning I realized how much I needed my husband's support. Yet I also knew it wouldn't be enough unless I allowed Jesus to heal my self-image.

When I returned home from the hospital, a well-meaning person came to our home. When she held out a hot dish, she allowed her gaze to fall. Her eye movement was so obvious that I was devastated. Even before she left, I prayed my John 20:23 prayer: "Jesus, in your name I forgive her. I ask you to bless her."

The moment she left, I fled to my bedroom, and tears came in a flood. In a new way I realized that the concentration of our culture upon a beautiful body had influenced my thinking at a deep level. Never perfect before, I now fell even farther short of the standard "they" had set for me. Yet my instinctive resentment was not directed against the culture that places a difficult burden on both beautiful and less-than-beautiful people. Perhaps that would have been easier. Instead hovering about me was the temptation to believe that I had failed by not being all that our culture sees as ideal.

For most of us self-esteem is tied into our perception of ourselves. That means paying attention to the feelings that may or may not be based in reality. As I adjusted to having a mastectomy, I found it especially important to take more time than usual in trying to look good.

Then with chemotherapy I started losing my hair. In many ways I found that even more difficult than a mastectomy. I lost my hair gradually over a period of time, and it became a constant chipping away at my morale.

So, too, did my memory of the woman's glance, for each time I went somewhere I met the same appraisal from other women. One day, while getting ready to go out, I felt as if I were going through an assembly line: Shampoo my thinning hair and hope it doesn't all vanish down the drain. Put on the prosthesis. Wig. Face paint. After all, I couldn't allow any pallor to hint that I might not feel well. And then I started to weep.

Standing in front of the mirror, I prayed, "Jesus, in your name I forgive myself for the way I am." In other words, "Jesus, in your name I forgive myself for the way I look in spite of my best efforts to be otherwise. I forgive myself for not being all that our culture says I should be."

Tears still in my eyes, I kept praying. "Thank you that you love me the way I am." I asked Jesus to fill me with his love and peace—to touch my emotional wounds and make me whole. With such a prayer I am not the one who has the power to forgive myself, nor to bring healing. The power comes in the name and person of Jesus Christ. He is the one who changes the depths of my spirit, bringing acceptance.

I didn't realize I had received healing about my appearance until a few weeks after my prayer. When a woman obviously checked me over, it no longer hurt. Instead it struck me as funny. I thought, *If you can see something wrong with the way I look, more power to you!*

As time went on, I sensed the real depth of the wholeness Christ had given. Even as giving and receiving forgiveness are necessary for self-esteem, so is the knowledge that we are loved. We all enjoy the *feeling* of being loved, but the *knowledge* of being loved is even more important. That knowledge goes beyond our emotional ups and downs. Again I used my will to forgive those who hurt me and then prayed, "Jesus, in your name I ask for healing. Bind up all the ragged edges. Bring wholeness, okay?" Often God responded by giving a sense of well-being, but I also stored up verses in my memory bank to withdraw as needed: "I have loved you with an everlasting love" (Jer. 31:3).

Those who have suffered a deep loss know that the process of coming to wholeness may involve another step. Fourteen months after surgery I woke from a nightmare about my mastectomy. From past experience I knew if I began having nightmares in an area of my life, they would continue. "Lord, what shall I do about this?" I prayed. As I turned the situation over to him, he impressed me with the thought, "Lois, I've healed your conscious mind. Your nightmare came from the subconscious."

That was the help I needed, for I remembered Luke 10:19: "Behold, I have given you authority to tread upon serpents and scorpions, and over all the power of the enemy; and nothing shall hurt you." Out of that leading I prayed, "Lord Jesus Christ, in your name I take authority over my subconscious thoughts. Heal any remaining hurt I've pushed down and submerged. Reveal to me your love." In subsequent months I had no further nightmares about my mastectomy.

What about Sex?

How can a life-changing surgery affect the intimate relationship between a husband and wife?

In every marriage it's important to remember that God gave sex as a gift, not only for procreation but also for a husband and wife to enjoy each other. It's part of God's plan that the marriage bed of a Christian couple be a holy place—a place where husband and wife grow in bonding together. Caring sexual intimacy between two Christians fulfills the words of Jesus when he said, "For this reason a man shall leave his father and mother and be joined to his wife, and the two shall become one" (Matt. 19:5).

Illness and life-changing accidents or disabilities do not have to change that relationship. If one of you is healthy and the other isn't, talk honestly abut the different needs you have. There may be times when you are physically able to have sex, but you may not feel like it, simply because chemotherapy or other medications slow down your body. Yet if you love one another, a mutual sense of giving will take you beyond initial difficulties.

In their book *Be Good to One Another*, Lowell and Carol Erdahl stress the importance of realizing that the experiences of sexual relations are not always the same:

Sometimes it's like having a seven-course candlelight dinner. At other times it's more like going to McDonald's for a hamburger. But what's so bad about that? As we can enjoy and be refreshed by both McDonald's and the finest restaurant, we can also enjoy and be enriched by a great variety of sexual experiences. Remembering this can free a couple from preoccupation with achieving supreme ecstasy in every encounter. Sexual relations can be beautiful in moods of play and fun and in more serene times of tender love.

For those who have experienced illness, life-changing accidents, or disabilities, I'd like to suggest a third image, partway between McDonald's and the finest restaurant. Think about the kind of bakery with a coffee shop on one side. When you come in, you go to a glass case, pick out your favorite goodie, and pour a cup of coffee. Then you sit down at a nearby table. The room is usually warmly decorated, the atmosphere cozy and comfortable. People come and go at the pace that's comfortable for them. It feels like a welcoming home.

If chemotherapy and medications slow down your usual sexual responses, be honest about it. But remember that your bedroom is a coffee shop, not a fast food place. No one is checking on how quickly you progress. As preparation for your lovemaking, set aside times when you feel most rested. Find low-key but interesting activities in which you can both participate. Find the pace that's comfortable as you move into intimacy.

If you feel performance oriented, remember you don't need to impress each other with the finest restaurant. Instead think about why you love each other. Think of the fun you've shared together, the tender moments both of you cherish. Remember that your husband or wife is your friend. In this moment of your lives neither of you has to perform.

The difference between lust and love is in being other-centered. Lust takes. Love gives. If it helps you as a woman, offer a silent prayer—"Lord, help me to have greater love for my husband than ever before." If it helps you as a man, offer the same prayer, or ask the Lord to help you be especially ten-der toward your wife. Remember how to give her pleasure.

True marital love involves cherishing each other—simply holding each other or being held when that is a comfort. Your marriage will deepen under such conditions.

In our sexually oriented society, it's easy to forget the value of words and the effect they have toward deepening love. One woman, in the hospital for a blood transfusion, was too weak to do anything but lie still. When visitors brought a small vase with a rose, baby's breath, and flowing white ribbon, she said, "Oh, it looks like a bride's bouquet."

But she received a greater gift from her husband. With his eyes on her he said, "I'm looking at a rose." For her it was a moment of being cherished.

During a women's retreat on wholeness of spirit, soul, and body, God answered my prayers by giving an additional revelation of his love. In the closing communion service, Luther Abrahamson spoke on Psalm 84:1: "How lovely is thy dwelling place, O Lord of hosts!" His words struck home: "You are the dwelling place of the Lord. You are lovely." Often I have repeated those words to myself, "I am the dwelling place of the Lord. I am lovely."

One evening my husband and I walked alongside a lake at sundown. Across the bay, fish leaped into the air—bodies arcing, then slapping the water as they fell back, creating ever-widening rings.

A ripple began as I accepted responsibility for myself and for what I am because of circumstances beyond my control. Because I knew Christ's love, I understood Paul's words in a life-giving way. "Do you not know that your body is a temple of the Holy Spirit within you, which you have from God? You are not your own; you were bought with a price. So glorify God in your body" (1 Cor. 6:19-20). The way I feel about my body becomes a means of revealing my faith. I want to look attractive, but even more, I want to live attractively.

As Christ enlarged the circle around me, I realized the depth of my healing. Never a raving beauty before, I am certainly not a beauty now. Never perfect before, I am definitely imperfect now. But because of what Christ has done for me, I regard myself as a whole person.

"You are the dwelling place of the Lord, Lois. You are lovely."

Pain understood by those who hold it with gentle hands becomes a precious bond.

FAITH THOUGHT

HOW LOVELY IS THY DWELLING PLACE, O LORD OF HOSTS! (Ps. 84:1)

> "How lovely is your dwelling place,"
> the psalmist sang,
> and I, too, am your dwelling place—
> a bit worn, in need of paint,
> at best, imperfect—
> but yes, Lord, your dwelling place.
> How lovely, how beautiful
> you make me
> because you live within!

CHAPTER FIFTEEN

LONESOME FOR HOME

In whatever way
I suffer loss
what can I learn
from those I love?
How can I know
the goodness of God?

DURING HER LAST ILLNESS, my friend Merriam told me, "Lois, your book *Either Way, I Win* doesn't go far enough." I knew what she meant. At the time I wrote the first edition, I had not lived long enough to take others beyond where I was. In the years since, I've walked through the valley of the shadow of death with a number of people—more than I can include in these pages. Each loved one has taught me about dying, about grieving, about helping others grieve. But most of all, each person has shown me something about how to live.

As Christians, we are united by our hope in the resurrection. Jesus told us, "I am the resurrection and the life; he who believes in me, though he die, yet shall he live, and whoever lives and believes in me shall never die" (John 11:25-26). By promising, "I go to prepare a place for you" (John 14:2), he gave us a destination.

That knowledge of heaven, that sense of going home to be with him and the Father, holds our lives together, even in the most desperate times. What can we learn from the serenity and anticipation of those who are lonesome for home? How can those who die more slowly help us deal with the fears in our own lives?

When I was on chemotherapy I dreaded the idea that illness might force me to be dependent on others. I didn't want my loved ones to have to face the chores involved in caring for a cancer patient. I didn't want friends and relatives to think, *Well, I better do my duty now and go visit Lois to cheer her up.*

At times I envied heart patients. I even heard one of them say, "I want to die with my boots on." He did. His honesty helped me speak more openly, to talk about things that matter, to ask questions that will count later on. I learned the meaning of the psalmist's words, "Precious in the sight of the Lord is the death of his saints" (Ps. 116:15). Always I'm struck by a thought that is another life principle:

> *The depth of our relationship with*
> *the Lord becomes most real in the*
> *moment when nothing else matters.*

None of us has the choice of how we will die, whether it be suddenly—healthy one moment, gone the next—or after a lingering illness. We may die while young, when middle-aged, or when full of years. We don't know whether we will be surrounded by loved ones or die alone.

But we do have a choice about something. The way we die will be influenced by the way we live. And the way we live will make it easier or more difficult for our loved ones to go on.

I soon realized that mature people who face the possibility of imminent death generally order their priorities. As they make their peace with God, a rare quality, a sense of peacefulness, comes into their spirit. When my dad entered a nursing home, staff members gathered to talk about his care. My sister Faith had the privilege of being there when a woman asked Dad, "Your records indicate that you don't want heroic efforts for resuscitation. Do you know what that means?"

"Yes," he answered, "I know what it means." He explained. "I've always loved to travel, and I expect that someday soon I'll take the greatest journey of all. I don't want anyone to mess with it."

As he told about his belief in Jesus Christ, the room fell quiet as each person listened intently, seemingly deeply moved.

Treasured Gifts

Those who experience cancer may have an advantage other people do not. Often cancer patients can be more intentional in the way they spend their last days. One man whose adult children lived in the same small town decided to make the most of the short amount of time he had left. Each morning his family gathered around, and they read Scripture and prayed together.

Another woman felt deeply concerned about the spiritual condition of some of the teenaged children in her extended family relationship. She spent long hours writing to them, talking by mail with them about what they needed to know and the choices they needed to make.

A grandmother named Elinor left a marked-up, often-used Bible for each of her six grandchildren. In each Bible was a careful inscription to the child for whom it was intended. The only thing missing was the date of Elinor's death.

Still others have actively prepared their children and other loved ones for what lay ahead. Because of surgery, Cindy was unable to speak in a normal way, but her daughter, Rachel, started learning sign language. The third of six children, Rachel taught her mother some simple signs to help communication between them. Months after her mother's death, Rachel told me that out of that beginning she wanted to go on to become an ASL interpreter.

A senior in high school, Rachel had taken the time to read my children's novels with her mother. Some of the novels have a deaf character who speaks in sign language. At her high school graduation party, Rachel talked to me about *The Fiddler's Secret*.

"It was the last book we read together," she said. "Mom really enjoyed it. It meant a lot to her."

Suddenly I remembered the theme of the book —"We know that in everything God works for good with those who love him, who are called according to his purpose."

"Oh!" I exclaimed. "Romans 8:28!"

Her eyes bright with memory, Rachel nodded and smiled.

Lonesome for Heaven

It was Cindy's sister-in-law, Julie, who taught me a phrase I've thought about ever since. Toward the end of her life, Cindy became lonesome for heaven.

What does it mean to feel lonesome for heaven? To walk closer and closer to the edge of death, to begin to separate yourself emotionally from this life in order to embrace the next?

When we moved to rural Wisconsin we discovered that there were four Lois Johnsons in our immediate area. One of them received my telephone calls so consistently that she kept my number next to her phone. Repeatedly she told callers, "Oh, you're looking for the Lois Johnson who writes and speaks." In her gracious way she never seemed to mind how often she passed on that message. Instead she laughed about being my personal secretary.

But there's something about Lois that I remember even more. When she died I joined her family for the visitation. It was the most startling trip I've ever made to a funeral home. In death Lois lived the words "fallen asleep in the Lord." She seemed to have taken a desired rest, a catnap to prepare her for the special time ahead. Though her eyes were closed, a trace of a smile remained. Her face seemed lit from within.

Lois looked as if she had just greeted someone she loved. As though her Lord had said, "Welcome home, my beloved child. Welcome home."

Seeing her expression, I felt curious. "How did Lois die?" I asked her son. "What was she doing?"

"She knew she was dying," he answered. "All day long and into the evening she lay in bed, singing hymns that she remembered. Repeating Bible verses she had memorized. And then, she simply slipped over to the other side."

There was no doubt that Lois was home. Her radiance even in death spoke one thing. She was with Jesus.

Often I've heard people describe that passage into heaven as a thin veil or a stepping into the next room. My cousin Betsy told how she and her sister stood next to their dying mother. "We just sang Mom into heaven."

Something to Remember Me By

My mother-in-law, Marie, came from Norway as a seventeen-year-old single girl. She met her future husband on the day he passed through Milwaukee, planning to return to the Old Country. Finding Marie changed his mind. He stayed in America.

During their thirty-four years of marriage, Marie and John lived in the two-bedroom lower half of a duplex. Somehow they squeezed six children and Marie's sister into that space. While living through the depression, they paid for their house three times but did not lose it. Yet when homeless men came to the door for a meal, Marie always fed them, saying, "We won't go hungry."

It came time for Marie, who by then was Mom Johnson to me, to leave that house for the last time. As she prepared to move to a new location, she gave away her possessions--to her own children and grandchildren, to the woman next door with sixteen children, to the young couple down the street who had just gotten married. When she closed the door of her home the final time, she had lived there over fifty years. But she never looked back.

Mom Johnson was eighty-five years old when she moved from Milwaukee to Minneapolis, and I asked her how it felt to leave all her friends behind.

"The first night I was here I sat myself down in a chair," she said. "I told myself, 'Marie, this is your home now. You're going to be happy here.' And I am."

Over the years Mom Johnson had crocheted afghans for each of her six children. Now, at eighty-five, she was working on the next generation. With thirteen grandchildren, that was no small feat. Whenever she gave one away, she said, "It's just something to remember me by."

When each grandchild had an afghan, she began crocheting bells and candy canes that adorned our Christmas trees. Each time a grandchild came to visit, she tucked a special belonging or something she had made into that child's hands. Mom had thought carefully about those gifts; they were always uniquely appropriate for the individual who received them. And always she'd say, "It's just something to remember me by."

Usually the grandkids protested. "Oh, Grandma, don't say that." Some of them no doubt wondered if she was thinking too much about her own death. Yet more than once I saw tears well up in the eyes of those busy young people who took time to visit her.

As Mom Johnson moved into designed living with part-time nursing care, she gave away her possessions in earnest. By now she had very little left, but even when she moved to full-time nursing care she still managed to find something to give to the grandchildren and great-grandchildren who came.

By then, as I heard her say, "Just something to remember me by," I, too, wondered about it. *Aren't we paying enough attention? Doesn't she feel our love?* Not until months later did I learn that in Old Country thinking it is the responsibility of the dying to help prepare their loved ones for that separation.

My precious mother-in-law, Mom Johnson, was nearly 101 years old when she died. During her last illness family members took turns, wanting to stay around the clock with her. As she lay with eyes closed, Roy and I heard her repeating the Norwegian word for Jesus under her breath.

The next time we came into the room, we discovered that she was not sleeping, as it appeared. She had just died, and we grieved that we missed her homegoing, probably by less than five minutes. A wise nurse told us, "You know those independent ones have a way of slipping away when they're alone."

Just the same, Mom Johnson had looked ahead, preparing us for this moment. On the day that she went home to Jesus, she had few earthly possessions left. But now when we look at the gifts she gave in love, we know we each received her special choice for us. We still hear her words, "It's just something to remember me by."

Commended to the Lord

One of my friends gave me something else. Over the years Martha had faithfully interceded for me. Then it was my turn to pray for her healing. One day, out of her spiritual maturity and a God-given sense, she told me when I needed to change the direction of my prayers. From that time on, Martha began preparing me, and I suspect others, for the separation we would face.

On my last visit to her apartment, there were several candles on her dresser. She pointed to the tall pillars shaped like a six-pointed star. "Pick out the color you like best," she said. "I made them awhile ago."

Deeply moved, I stared at them and thought, *Oh, Martha! It's a symbol for light even in the darkness.*

Then she said, "There's something else for you." She pointed to a large 16-by-21-inch wooden plaque leaning against the wall.

I took one look, and tears welled up in my eyes, for there was something Martha never knew. Years before, during my months on chemotherapy, I attended a meeting in the home of a woman named Mary. In her front hall hung a plaque exactly like this one. Boldly it proclaimed, "Be Aglow and Burning with the Spirit" (Rom. 12:11).

Seeing it, my spirit leaped, for that's how I wanted to reflect the Lord. *If I could ever find one just like that,* I thought to the Lord, *it would be such a great reminder of you.* Then I learned that the plaque was handmade by Mary's husband. As far as I knew, there wasn't another one like it. I forgot my wishful prayer, but not the message.

That day on my last trip to Martha's home, I learned that Mary's husband had made this plaque for Martha. And Martha, not knowing about my prayer, said to me, "I believe you're the one who's supposed to have it."

My next visit with Martha was in a hospital room. That day Martha told me about the funeral arrangements she and her husband had made. Having no doubt that this would be the last time I'd see her alive, I knelt on the floor next to her bed and prayed for her.

When I finished, she reached out, placed her hand on my head, and prayed, "Lois, I commend you to the Lord."

Down through the years her Old Testament kind of blessing has echoed in my heart whenever I needed those words. This woman who had so often brought me before the Lord did the best thing she possibly could while dying: "Lois, I put you into his hands. I give you his safekeeping. His shelter, his protection, his love, his leading for all the days ahead. His caring."

"Lois, I commend you to the Lord."

The Last Good-Bye

In times of illness and death we do our best to build memories. With my own mother, our family members stood around her bedside and sang every hymn and spiritual song we knew. We prayed together and felt that unity in the Lord. But then I left the room for just a few minutes to make up a bed for a tired relative. In that brief space of time, Mom slipped home.

I felt angry and frustrated, cheated because I was not with Mom for her last breath. After months of caregiving, why was I the one who missed that moment? I tried to tell myself, *I was doing what Mom always did. She had the gift of hospitality. She always took care of us.* It didn't work.

A friend told me, "Lois, the moment of death isn't any more sacred than other moments you'd had with your loved ones all along. Think about sharing a sandwich together, times you've had precious talks. Those moments are sacred too."

That helped me, but I knew I could never take for granted the pain of those who want a special time to remember. An unexpected death breaks into all of life. What about those who do not have the opportunity to give any kind of good-bye?

Because of my friend's encouragement, I asked myself, *What were the most special moments I had with my mother?* I remembered the warm summer day I wheeled her chair outside. As we talked together, we sat under tall trees, enjoying the shade. "Mom, are you at peace with the Lord?" I asked.

"Oh, yes!" she exclaimed. "I don't talk a lot about my faith, but all day long and when I wake up during the night I sense that he is with me."

When my sister-in-law Helen died alone, I grieved that no one was with her. But then a friend wrote, saying, "I felt sad to think that she was alone when she died, but I guess that's from our perspective on this side of eternity. She certainly wasn't alone in death. I know the Lord was with her."

No longer do I believe there is a veil between life and death. Nor is there a stepping into the next room. For those who boldly proclaim, "I know whom I have believed," Christ comes right into the room.

For years I visited my elderly father in a nursing home. Toward the end of his life, he suffered from Parkinson's disease. As I drove the sixty miles one way to see him, I asked the Lord to make Dad's mind clear so we could visit together. Sometimes God honored that prayer. Other times he used different ways to make my visits meaningful.

On a day five months after Mom died, Dad spoke with surprising clarity about how much he missed her and their days of traveling together with a trailer. Then we talked about the early verses of John 14 where Jesus promises to prepare a place for us.

"Someday soon you'll get to go and be with Mom," I said. "In that great big house in heaven you can share the same room and be together again."

A sudden grin lit my father's eyes. "And there will be a trailer out in the parking lot."

In the next breath he began reciting from memory John 14:1-6. He spoke in a clear voice, stronger than it had been in months, not missing one word.

Soon after, Dad lapsed into a month-long period of not being able to communicate. I began to pray that I could be with my dad when he died. More than once I prayed that I would know when I should drop everything to see him. When the Lord impressed me to visit him on a Thursday morning, Roy and I drove out together.

When we entered Dad's room, the nurse said, "Did your father know you were coming? He's been asking for you."

Really? I thought, glad we had come on a day when he was clear.

In that moment Dad reached out, took Roy's arm, and said, "Take me to the top of the hill. I want to go home. I know the Way." That day Dad got up for breakfast and lunch, but those were his last words to us. Thirty-six hours later, I sensed that I should drop everything and drive back to see him. When I arrived, a nurse saw me pass the station. "Lois, I was just going to call you and ask you to come. Your dad is slipping."

As he lay in a deep sleep, I stayed with him through the night. I sat in his room in the chair next to his bed and thought about the years we had spent together. Believing he could still hear, I read or recited Bible verses to him. I deeply cherished this man.

Morning came, and Dad was still alive. Roy joined me, and as a family, we gathered in Dad's room, talked, prayed, came and went. Dad continued to rest comfortably in a deep sleep.

While others stayed, Roy and I went out for lunch. As soon as we returned, the others left, and the nurse asked us to step out of the room while she took care of Dad. Coming back again, we moved over to Dad's bedside to stand next to him as he slept.

Less than a minute later, Dad opened his eyes, but it was not us he was seeing. When I realized what was happening, my words tumbled out. "Oh, Dad, Jesus is waiting for you. He's holding open his arms for you. Just run into his arms!"

Together Roy and I prayed the Lord's Prayer. By the time we finished, Dad was home. Remembering how he and Mom always closed their devotions, I prayed the benediction for them.

Now when we go to the final resting place of my parents, we visit a cemetery at the top of a hill. As I stand next to their gravestone, I look across the street to the tall steeple of a church my father once served as pastor. Then I look down to the words etched in the back side of the granite: "JESUS SAID, 'I AM THE WAY, AND THE TRUTH, AND THE LIFE; NO ONE COMES TO THE FATHER, BUT BY ME.'" JOHN 14:6.

"Take me to the top of the hill," Dad said. "I want to go home. I know the Way."

FAITH THOUGHT

JESUS CAME AND TOUCHED THEM, SAYING, "RISE, AND HAVE NO FEAR." AND WHEN THEY LIFTED UP THEIR EYES, THEY SAW NO ONE BUT JESUS ONLY. (MATT. 17:7-8)

Too often I wait
with building memories
until they must of necessity
become memorials.
Help me, Lord,
to create moments
of joy or tenderness,
laughter or silence,
listening or sharing my heart—
moments as valued as drops of dew
because they vanish as quickly.
Help me, Lord,
to create moments that live on
when the person I love
is home with you.

THE SEASON OF SINGING

———◆◆———

Strange, Lord.
Why are you always bigger
than I begin to guess?
Why are you always stronger,
yet so gentle
that your powerful touch
passes over me
as a breath of hope?

ON GOOD FRIDAY, editor Roger Palms left his desk at *Decision* magazine to come to my hospital room. There he, my husband, and I bowed our heads together. "Lord, you have created Lois," Roger prayed. "Now we ask you to re-create her."

In the months that followed, I thought of his words often. Because of Christ's death on a Good Friday long ago, I had been re-created through salvation. Now he was to give me new life in other ways.

Spring came to our part of the country a few weeks after my surgery. One day I sat in my car, resting and waiting for a class to begin. From that hillside I looked down over budding trees. Still tightly folded, the buds formed a soft green against the sky, a promise of the full leaf to come.

"Lord," I prayed. "You re-create the earth each spring. Surely you can re-create me."

Soon I discovered that re-creation involved a physical process, for with each new leaf, each added bit of strength, I felt springtime in my heart. But there was more. The word *re-creation* became a checkpoint—a way for me to evaluate my past and think about how I wanted to live in whatever time I had left.

In his Song of Songs, Solomon writes, "See! The winter is past; the rains are over and gone. Flowers appear on the earth; the season of singing has come" (2:11-12 NIV).

When God adds life to the days we thought might be over, we experience the rains. We see flowers appear and know that his season of singing has come. What are some truths that will help all of us experience God's re-creation? What thoughts can we hold close and remember? Here are some ideas.

1) *You are called by God.*
On a warm spring day when I was nine and a half years old, I was even more naughty than usual, and my mother needed to discipline me. I was too tender emotionally for a spanking and had an older sister who always said, "Spank me quick so I can run back out and play."

Nor could my mother send me to my room. I would simply read a book, and that would not be punishment. So she asked me to clean the leaves out of the barberry bushes in front of our house.

It was a prickly job, scratching my hands and trying my patience. As I sat down on a sidewalk warmed by spring sunlight, the church bell in our small town began to ring. I knew that someone had died and counted the long tolls echoing across the countryside: eighty-nine, ninety, ninety-one. Then they stopped.

What a long time for someone to live, I thought. *I wonder what that person left behind. I wonder what I'll leave behind.*

I didn't think about the gifts of love and kindness every one of us can leave for others. Instead there was one thing I wanted to do. If I could possibly write a book, that's what I wanted to leave behind. I wanted that book to tell others what I believed about Jesus Christ.

From then on I took my call from God seriously. That evening I went up to my room to start my first novel. Though I was nine and a half years old, I continued working on that novel night after night.

Years later, I still feel grateful for God's strong leading, but now I know two secrets: The grace of being called to a life's work while being disciplined for doing something wrong. And the certainty that without him I can do nothing.

You see, this is the book I was writing when diagnosed with cancer. More than any other I've written, this was the book I wanted to finish. If I was not going to live, this was the book I wanted to leave behind.

We don't have to know God's call on our lives at nine years old. Nor do we need to know it at twelve, or fifteen. The important thing to remember is that if we are open to it, God will show us what he wants us to do.

Because of cancer, the direction of this book changed dramatically, even as my life changed. I discovered another life principle:

If we look to Jesus
in every circumstance,
he sets us free to serve.

With that principle comes another truth that helps us experience his re-creation.

2) *Your value isn't in what you have or do, but in belonging to him.*

In *Make your Illness Count* Vernon Bittner made me aware of a way in which my need to control had to be relinquished. He talks about the false guilt people experience when illness curtails work. I was no exception. As a cancer patient, I wanted to do everything I possibly could by myself, but that, too, needed to be kept in balance.

While recuperating from my mastectomy, I found it difficult to keep the house as clean as I would like. Washing clothes grew from a two-hour task to an all-day one. Vacuuming was hardest of all. But more painful than housecleaning was the false guilt accompanying my attempts. As with others in crisis, I found my view of self diminishing. I told myself, *I can't do as much work, so I'm not worth anything as a wife and mother.*

As I realized what was happening, I prayed, "Lord, release me from this false guilt."

Only a few days later I had forgotten my prayer. Determined to overcome after-surgery weakness, I decided not to wait until Roy or our sons could help. To prove myself, I vacuumed the living room. By the time I came to the kitchen, I felt light-headed. Turning off the vacuum, I leaned over the counter, too weak to reach a chair five feet away. Resting there, I heard the radio from the living room.

Inspirational music filled the air, then stopped. A speaker began, and the essence of his message was Christ saying to me, "Lois, I love you, not for what you can do, but for who you are, and because of what you mean to me."

Out of the strength of that moment, I decided, *If Jesus feels that way about me, my family does also.*

The answer to my prayer came in two ways. First, I began to see that my efforts to work, even when detrimental to my health, were really a combination of pride and guilt, an insistence upon being in control. "And Lois, you don't need to be," my Lord seemed to be saying. "I'm the one who's supposed to be in control."

The second answer was practical. Neither of our sons had part-time jobs then, and my husband and I decided to raise their allowances a small amount. I sat down with them, making two lists of tasks that needed to be accomplished each week. I asked them to do more than usual, and I included chores I found especially difficult. They agreed to the lists and alternated them biweekly for a change of pace.

When I saw their willingness, I thought, *How ridiculous! Why didn't I do that long ago?* In the days that followed, my false guilt and need to be in control lifted, because I did not have to continually ask for help.

"Lois, I love you, not for what you can do, but for who you are, and because of what you mean to me."

3) The Lord can use your sense of inadequacy.

A prideful self-sufficiency keeps many of us from being used. My sense of inadequacy has hindered me even more. In *Bless My Growing*, Gerhard Frost reminds us of something important:

> *Only he who stands in awe can be trusted with a great and difficult task. . . . It is well to be prepared, but we dare not forget that we are never fully prepared for the tasks that are most worth doing. The tasks that are worthy of us, as persons, are often beyond us.*

A sense of inadequacy about the task confronting me becomes an asset if it forces me to turn to God and seek wisdom. In a time of need the Lord has made me freshly aware of the equipping of members in the body of Christ:

> *So we are to use our different gifts in accordance with the grace that God has given us. If our gift is to speak God's message, we should do it according to the faith that we have; if it is to serve, we should serve; if it is to teach, we should teach; if it is to encourage others, we should do so. Whoever shares with others should do it generously; whoever has authority should work hard; whoever shows kindness to others should do it cheerfully.* (Rom. 12:6-8 TEV)

When that passage struck me, I wanted to learn more about my spiritual gifts, then use them in the body of Christ. I felt encouraged that others can provide balance for areas I lack. I did not need to function in all of the gifts; I only needed to surrender the ones I have.

Because I am a Christian, the Holy Spirit had already given me the potential to be used in any of his gifts. Yet I was spreading myself too thin. When torn in every direction, I prayed, "Lord, reveal to me the spiritual gifts you have given me. In your name I ask you to release them."

I began noticing what areas of Christian service I particularly enjoyed. God wants us happy in the way we serve him. As I listened to him, I saw that if I worked within an area of giftedness, my usefulness increased.

When the Lord wants to use us in a certain way he gives us that desire. We not only experience joy but also more energy and persistence in that area of service. I return home feeling rested, and my gifts are confirmed through the responses of those around me.

4) *Nothing in your life will be wasted.*

During a discouraged moment I talked with a person who had often prayed for my healing: "If I don't live, I hope you won't feel responsible for the way our prayers are answered," I said. "We have simply prayed together."

The reply was immediate: "You mean I'm not supposed to feel bad if you die?"

In that instant I understood how ridiculous I was being. While I did not want to worry people, I would feel terrible if they did not care.

At the same time I didn't like being in the position of making people feel anxious. For many years I had felt a necessity to stay well for my husband's sake, because he had lost his first wife through illness. I didn't want him to experience that pain again.

To a certain extent it's possible to be healthy by taking care of myself. In another sense I can never guarantee I'll be well, any more than my husband can promise to be healthy for me.

As I thought about it, I remembered a hand-lettered Christmas card we received from Tom Swedien and his family. Tom quoted from the second chapter of Philippians:

> *The attitude you should have is the one that Christ Jesus had:*
> *He always had the nature of God, but he did not think that by*
> *force he should try to become equal with God. Instead of this, of*

his own free will he gave up all he had, and took the nature of
a servant. He became like man and appeared in human likeness.
He was humble and walked the path of obedience all the way to
death—his death on the cross. (Phil. 2:5-8 TEV)

Tom went on to write: "But keep Advent near . . . remembering
that *because He gave it all up, we can grasp it,* and walking in obedience come to fully realize what life is really about."

God does not waste pain. He will use whatever we've learned
from him about servanthood to help us comfort others. Because
he gave it all up, we can grasp it.

5) *Jesus understands your need for power.*

Andrew Murray writes, "Prayer not only teaches and strengthens
[us] to work: work teaches and strengthens [us] to pray." Out of
my need for inspiration in my work, I learned the creativity and
power available through prayer.

For some time I had struggled, not wanting to give the Lord
permission to work in every area of my life. As I fought the
Spirit's gentle voice, I felt nothing but demands and pressure in
my home and vocational responsibilities. That sense of living
under tension, unable to find joy and satisfaction in what I was
doing, forced me to realize how I limited God. "Lois, you're trying to work in your own power," he impressed on me in various
ways. "Let me give you mine."

In Ephesians 1:18-20 NIV, Paul asks the God of our Lord
Jesus Christ to give the Spirit of wisdom and revelation so that we
may know him better:

I pray also that the eyes of your heart may be enlightened in
order that you may know the hope to which he has called you,
the riches of his glorious inheritance in the saints, and his
incomparably great power for us who believe. That power is like
the working of his mighty strength, which he exerted in Christ
when he raised him from the dead and seated him at his right
hand in the heavenly realms, far above all rule and authority,

power and dominion, and every title that can be given, not only in the present age but also in the one to come.

If we take those words seriously, we have access to the level of power that raised Christ from the dead. If that's true, then why didn't I have that power?

As I prayed about my situation, I realized what I was really saying to God: "It's all right for you to be Lord in certain areas of my life. But there's at least three other areas where I don't want you."

One morning I talked to a pastor about my spiritual and emotional blockages and my feeling that I couldn't teach prayer seminars anymore. That day he prayed, "Lord, take away the burden Lois senses in her speaking and writing. Make it easier for her to work." When I heard his words, I was able to pray, "Lord, make me willing to grow. Thank you for all you're going to do in my life."

As soon as I left his office, my mind took over, again fighting God. Deep down, however, I knew how much I needed help in my work and witness. At two o'clock in the morning the Spirit spoke to my subconscious, bringing me awake, washing over me with love, peace, and joy. Gone was my reluctance to grow. I had received the power I needed.

Jesus never intended his disciples to witness without that power and authority. When they locked the doors for fear of the Jews, Jesus stood among them, saying, "As the Father has sent me, so I send you." Then he breathed on them and said, "Receive the Holy Spirit" (John 20:19-22).

In his final instructions to his disciples, Jesus said, "And behold, I send the promise of my Father upon you; but stay in the city, until you are clothed with power from on high" (Luke 24:49). In Acts 1:8, he told them again: "But you shall receive power when the Holy Spirit has come upon you; and you shall be my witnesses in Jerusalem and in all Judea and Samaria and to the end of the earth."

Historically that power came upon the disciples on the day of Pentecost (Acts 2). We personally receive that power in direct proportion to how dependent we are on the Lord. He gives us only as much power as we're willing to receive.

If you, too, need more power in your life, study the Scripture passages about the work of the Holy Spirit. Ask forgiveness for your sins. Renounce any unholy spirit. Affirm your belief in Jesus Christ as your Savior and Lord. Ask Jesus to release in you *all* the power of his Holy Spirit. Thank him in faith by speaking the words he gives you.

6) *As you sow generously, the Lord will bring the harvest.*

It's the Lord's responsibility to bring the harvest, not ours. In *Times to Remember* Rose Fitzgerald Kennedy tells how she liked to quote from the book of Luke to her children: "To whom much has been given, much will be required" (Luke 12:48). From that upbringing came the words of her son, President John F. Kennedy: "And so, my fellow Americans: ask not what your country can do for you—ask what you can do for your country."

In 2 Corinthians 9, Paul writes, "He who sows sparingly will also reap sparingly, and he who sows bountifully will also reap bountifully. . . . He who supplies seed to the sower and bread for food will supply and multiply your resources and increase the harvest of your righteousness" (vv. 6, 10). When we feel that nothing is happening, we may need to wait for God's long view and leave eternal results up to him.

As I continued with chemotherapy, I tried to sow encouragement into the lives of others, but my questions multiplied. Finally, after the funeral of a woman I loved, I walked out to the church parking lot. Relieved to have a few moments alone, I stood next to my car and looked up. "Lord," I prayed, "why have you allowed me to live when others have died?" It was not a question I asked lightly.

That day I needed God's reminder that he knows the time of my death (Ps. 139:16). Because of free will, carelessness, or refusing to take care of myself, I could shorten my life needlessly. But if I cooperate with him and live as he desires, I allow him to decide the time of my homegoing. However short or long those years are, I want to use them wisely.

No matter what form of suffering we face, it changes us forever. The things we notice, the values we care about, the people we remember are all part of our new lives.

After the first edition of this book was published, I heard a story so often that I knew what the ending would be before I heard it. The story changed only with the name and relationship of the person who died.

"Lois, I want to tell you something," someone began. "After the funeral of my loved one I went back to clean up his room. Dad's Bible lay on the bedside table. On top of his Bible was your book. It was placed as though Dad wanted to give me a final message—*Either way, I win.*"

Every person who has told me that story received comfort in knowing how their loved one felt about dying. Listening to them, I felt grateful to God for the way he had used the book. But I also thought of the person who died.

Smart lady! I'd tell myself. Or, *Wise man! Even in death, you brought comfort to your loved ones.*

In the years after being diagnosed with cancer I started writing historical mystery novels to help children know the Lord. In the plots I blend the lives of my fictional characters with those of people who actually lived in that time. Sometimes those people are famous. Most of the time they were known only in the locale in which they lived. Yet, though I went back nearly 100 years for the Adventures of the Northwoods series and 150 years for the Riverboat Adventures, I discovered an amazing consistency. While researching sixteen novels in six states, I met only one exception to a rule. I had absolutely no problem finding out what kind of a person someone was and what he or she stood for.

By contrast, I've talked with countless people about the deaths of their loved ones. It takes only two sentences for them to share their heart's cry. When I ask, "Was your loved one a Christian?" many answer, "Yes, I'm grateful to say that he was."

Others tell me, "On his deathbed he made peace with the Lord." But still others say, "I don't know. I just wish I did."

With the last group there is always deep sadness in their eyes because, of course, they know but don't want to say it. I've been heartbroken by the cry of children and teenagers who asked me, "Where is my grandma?" or, "Where is my daddy?" I've grieved with adult children who simply said, "If only I knew."

The longing of their hearts has given me a deep desire. When my time comes to die, I want to be sure that my loved ones know exactly where I've gone. I want them to know not only because of my conversation but also by what I've written down. I want to leave behind notebooks and scraps of paper, written-in Bibles, and any other evidence that would convict me before a courtroom filled with jurors needing to decide whether I was a Christian.

In the Old Testament accounts of the kings of Israel and Judah, their lives are often summed up in one sentence: "Asa's heart was fully committed to the Lord all his life." Or, "He [Amaziah] did what was right in the eyes of the Lord, but not wholeheartedly." Or, "He [Jehoram] passed away, to no one's regret" (2 Chron. 5:17; 25:2; 21:20 NIV).

When God calls me home, I hope I will have lived in such a way that I can be remembered with one sentence: "Lois Walfrid Johnson followed the Lord wholeheartedly all the days of her life."

No extra clauses. No partial sentences because there was something I kept between myself and the Lord. Just "Lois Walfrid Johnson followed the Lord wholeheartedly all the days of her life."

You see, it all comes down to one thing—Christ's words in John 12:32: "And I, when I am lifted up from the earth, will draw all men to myself."

7) You can live with your eye on the clock of eternity.

When we experience a life-threatening diagnosis of cancer, our perspective changes. If the course of our illness goes well, we enter the stream of life again. We may forget where we have been for a moment, a day, or even a week. Yet seldom do we ever again take time for granted.

As the years slipped away, my husband and I had concerns, not just about our own children but for the next generation of his side of the family. Except for the two sons born to Roy and me, every child in that generation had lost a parent at a young age.

While driving to the funeral of his youngest brother, Roy and I talked about it. We wanted these kids we loved so much to know one another in some setting other than a funeral. We wanted them to come together and simply have fun. And so, we planned our first-ever reunion for that side of the family. We needed to create our own season of singing.

Our loved ones came from across the country to our country home for a weekend. We did, indeed, have fun. They shared their hearts and we shared ours. We talked and played together. And we learned the glory of these young adults who had lost so much. We saw that in spite of all their loss—or because of it—they had grown straight and strong and true.

On Saturday evening we sat around a campfire, singing one song after another. With some of those songs we laughed; others united our hearts in the fellowship of cherished memories. Then, while the dusk gathered around us, our nephew John stood up. Tall in stature, big of heart and voice, he began singing "How Great Thou Art."

As his voice filled the quiet country air, John suddenly stretched out his hand, telling us to turn. Behind us, two does and their fawns bounded across the field and up a hill. Moments later they disappeared toward the setting sun. *Oh, God, how great thou art!*

When Jesus called his disciples together, he did not evade the issue. He wanted to know how they were coming along spiritually. "Who do people say the Son of Man is?" he asked.

"Some say John the Baptist; others say Elijah; and still others, Jeremiah or one of the prophets."

"But what about you?" Jesus asked. "Who do you say that I am?" (Matt. 16:13-16).

With each of us Jesus asks that same question: "Who do you say that I am?"

Can we answer with Peter, "You are the Christ, the Son of the living God"?

Can we join Paul's bold declaration in Romans 14:7-8 TEV? "None of us lives for himself only, none of us dies for himself only. If we live, it is for the Lord that we live, and if we die, it is for the Lord that we die. So whether we live or die, we belong to the Lord."

Either way, you win. Either way, I win. Whatever happens to us, we belong to the Lord.

"The winter is past; the rains are over and gone. Flowers appear on the earth; the season of singing has come."

Oh, God, how great thou art!

Lord, you have given me
a new song to sing!
Though the time ahead
stretches into the unknown,
I go forward filled with hope,
knowing you conduct the symphony
of the present and the future.
In my body, soul, and spirit,
you composed a melody;
In the discords of my life
you brought harmony.
I rejoice, Lord, I praise you!
Make me an alleluia
of your redeeming grace,
your everlasting love,
your overcoming power.

STUDY GUIDE
AND DISCUSSION
QUESTIONS

———◆———

A S I LOOK BACK ON THE WRITING OF *Either Way, I Win,* my mind keeps returning to Oklahoma City and the image of the tall, white-robed Christ who weeps with us. It's my prayer that within the pages of this book you see Jesus in a new way—that your experience of suffering brings you closer to him. Whether you're a new believer or a long-time Christian, you have the opportunity to use your difficult times for growth in him.

If you read this book by yourself, set your own pace for these study questions. If the Lord gives you a special thought, stop there. Linger over it. Write it down. Let it go deep into your spirit. The next day return to the place where you left off.

If instead you meet with a discussion group, adapt the number of sessions according to what works for your group. I've given an option of meeting together for eight weeks. If that's too long, make it three weeks, or six, or whatever. Combine chapters as needed or take longer on a topic. Decide where you wish to put your emphasis. You may, for instance, want to spend more time on the three healing chapters—12, 13, and 14—and less time somewhere else. Or you may wish to spend more than one session on chapter 7, "Prayer That Makes a Difference."

As you discuss the study questions, be sensitive to individual differences. Allow others to find their comfort level in what they want to share. Though your experiences are not identical, you'll find that suffering brings common denominators. Whatever a cancer patient learns about dealing with fear, for instance, can be helpful to a single mom who faces an uncertain future and the rearing of three children.

However you use this guide, start by reading the Scripture verses at the beginning of each set of questions. Join in a brief prayer, asking for the Lord's presence, and your fellowship will take on a richer dimension. Pray again as you end your time together. Bring individual and group needs to Jesus and let him help you.

If you use a notebook as a prayer journal, you'll be able to go back to your key thoughts and be renewed by that nourishment. You'll remember how the Spirit of Jesus spoke to you. You'll recall those moments of grace you want to cherish and hold forever.

You'll also find a pack of three-by-five cards a good tool. On one side write the Scripture verse the Lord has made real. On the other side keep track of the need or reason why that verse spoke to you. Add the date. Before long, you'll have a history of your own unique walk with the Lord.

Whoever you are and no matter how good or difficult your circumstances, remember a life-giving certainty: Jesus stands with his arms open, ready for you to walk into them. As you look up into his face, what choices do you want to make?

Session 1: Face the Challenge

Preface: Dear Friend

1. *Read Exodus 2:1-21:* In what kind of lifestyle did Moses grow up? Compare the kind of person Moses probably was with someone you know today. Contrast the way Moses probably lived in Egypt with the way he lived in Midian.

2. Exodus 3:1 tells us that Moses was on the far side of the desert. What practical reason brought him there? How is "the far side of the desert" spiritually significant?

3. When God spoke from a burning bush (Exod. 3:1-10), what did he ask Moses to do? How did Moses respond (Exod. 3:11-13)? How do his responses compare with what he might have said if still living in Egypt? What reasons can you give for the change?

4. For the rest of Exodus chapter 3 and chapter 4:1-17, God continues to either challenge Moses or offer comfort. What help does God promise? What challenges? Describe the responses Moses gives in Exodus 4:1, 10, and 13. How will his attitude become important when Moses returns to Egypt? When he leads the Israelites into the wilderness?

5. Lois was diagnosed with the kind of cancer seen under a microscope, but she mentions other forms of cancer. Name some of them. How can these kinds of "cancer" become a desert experience for each one of us?

6. What "cancer" or "desert" have you experienced? Is there a way in which you're suffering right now? How have you changed because of this experience? Describe the attitudes and practical ways of coping that you've learned. How is God using those changes for good?

7. In Exodus 3:12, God promised Moses, "I will be with you." Why do those words offer comfort to you? If God has given you a similar promise, tell what it is and how it helped you.

To pray about:
   In whatever desert you live, invite Jesus to reveal himself to you.

Chapter 1: Trouble Ahead

1. *Read Luke 22:31-32:* How would you describe the feeling of being sifted like wheat? In what ways have you felt sifted? What is the difference between feeling sifted and facing something really traumatic?

2. Think about a moment that changed your life forever. It's painful to remember the instant when you receive bad news. Yet

facing that crisis helps you begin the steps toward healing. How does suffering—whatever it involves—change your perspective?

3. How did Lois's perception of time change? What happens when we can no longer take time for granted? When even moments become sacred?

4. In this and each of the chapters that follow, think about the kernel of truth called a life principle. Study the faith thoughts — they are verse you may want to memorize so you can recall them day or night.

5. Are you searching for God in your suffering? If so, be honest about it. If he has already helped you in a moment of crisis and the days that followed, tell about it. Describe how God has helped you see what is important.

To pray about:

As you face a moment that changed your life forever, ask Jesus to wrap his arms around you.

Chapter 2: Walk Out of Fear

1. *Read Isaiah 43:1-3a:* As with any verse that God uses to help you, read it aloud if you're in a place where that's possible. Look at the first line of verse 1. Who is speaking to you? How does that add impact to the meaning of the verse?

2. Why is a cancer patient especially vulnerable to fear? Why does fear plague every one of us, no matter what illness or stress we face?

3. In what ways does fear make you a prisoner? List the four questions that can help you deal with the initial impact of the crisis or suffering you face.

4. "Fear not," said the angel to startled shepherds on a quiet hillside. "Be not afraid, for behold, I bring you good news of a great joy which will come to all the people; for to you is born this day in the city of David a Savior, who is Christ the Lord" (Luke 2:10-11). Do you have some favorite "Fear not" verses? Check out just a few of God's promises: Isaiah 41:10, 13; 2 Timothy 1:7; Romans 8:15; 1 John 4:18; Psalm 23:4; Genesis 15:1; 26:24.

Choose a verse that is especially meaningful to you or use a concordance and search out one of your own. Write it down or, even better, memorize it.

5. Do you believe that fear can give you a reason to grow? Why or why not?

To pray about:
   In the midst of reasons for fear, ask God to help you grow.

Session 2: Lay the Foundation

Chapter 3: Standing Up When Feeling Down

1. *Read Romans 15:4-6, 13; and Matthew 14:13:* When you face a chasm in your life, you desperately need a bridge across. God offers you the cables of Scripture and prayer. How can you make his resources part of your daily life?

2. John Sherrill explained how he received God's help in his daily Bible reading. When he talks about illuminated verses, what does he mean? If you've had this kind of experience, how would you describe what happened?

3. When you face a crisis or long-term suffering, on what do you concentrate? What ideas help you in such a time? How has the Lord given you his specific encouragement?

4. A young mother said, "I want my children to be comfortable with silence." Why did Jesus draw away and leave the crowds behind? Go back to the first twelve verses of Matthew 14 and see why Jesus was deeply troubled. How can your willingness to pull back or draw away be necessary in your spiritual life?

5. Give the four steps for standing up when you're feeling down. Talk about how to use each step. Consider how to apply those ideas in your daily life.

6. Oswald Chambers has said, "God does not give us overcoming life—He gives us life as we overcome." Overcoming usually does not happen in one big leap but rather step-by-step. Describe how that has been true for you.

7. What is the difference between having faith in faith and having faith in God and his promises? Remember to study the life principles in each chapter. They offer kernel-of-truth faith points.

To pray about:
> In whatever you face, ask God to help you establish a pattern of taking him at his word.

Chapter 4: Free to Live!

1. *Read John 1:14; and Ephesians 2:8-9:* How do you define grace? Can you remember times when God has shown his grace in your life? In what ways did he help you?

2. What are some of the reasons that keep people from coming to peace about what will happen to them after death? Are these reasons valid? Why or why not?

3. In *View from a Hearse* Joe Bayly writes, "The paradox is that when you accept the fact of death, you are freed to live." What does it mean to face and accept the fact of death? How can you know without doubt that you are free to live? Review the Bible verses that helped Lois be certain about her personal salvation in Jesus Christ.

4. Can you be certain that you have eternal life? If you aren't sure, ask the Lord to speak to you through the salvation verses given in chapter 4 or in whatever way he chooses. As you read 1 John 5:13-15, underline the word *know.* Is this certainty of eternal life dependent on faith or feelings? Explain your answer.

5. In what ways do you need to make your peace with the Lord? What does it mean to drive your stake in the ground?

To pray about:
> If you do not know Jesus, confess your sin and ask him to be your Savior and Lord. If you do know Jesus, confess and ask forgiveness for any sin that would keep you from going on with him.

Session 3: Find the Tools

Chapter 5: The Gift of Communication

1. *Read Romans 8:35-39:* Every one of us wants to feel that we are a conqueror. Yet trouble and hardship can make us feel separated from the love of Christ. A husband described something that happened to his wife—a woman who is normally very verbal and quick to express her feelings. "She was so upset about what happened that she couldn't even speak." Why is it hard for all of us to talk about the things that hurt us deeply?

2. How can difficult times make us feel far away from the love of Jesus? What is your first reaction when a crisis rears its ugly head? In what ways do you try to hide? How do you avoid talking about what really bothers you?

3. What is anticipatory grief? There are times when we need to live by faith instead of feelings. There are other times when we need to go beyond what we think to what we feel. When we are dealing with difficult times, why is it necessary to recognize our feelings?

4. What is a "protect your spouse" game? (This can also be a "protect *anyone* who cares about you" problem.) Why do we play the biggest games with the people we love the most? How can a lack of communication hurt you?

5. When the enemy wants to defeat us, he tries to make us feel separated and alone. He does his best to make us think that no one cares. How can our unwillingness to talk about what is happening lead us into depression? What is a one-sentence definition of depression?

6. Describe some healthy ways to talk about anger and other hard-to-communicate feelings. What role does forgiveness play in healthy communication? What words can you use to communicate your forgiveness to someone else?

7. Is it okay to ignore people who continually drag you down? Why or why not? Who are the replenishers in your life? Why do you like being around them? In what ways do they build you up?

To pray about:

> *Thank God for his carefully chosen people in your life. If you don't have such people, ask the Lord for them.*

Chapter 6: All Things, Lord?

1. Read Mark 15:33-34. Read Romans 8:28, 31-34 in as many versions and paraphrases as you have available to you.

2. List the five stages of grief identified by Dr. Elisabeth Kübler-Ross in her book *On Death and Dying.* Why is it essential to go through the stages of grief?

3. Why does it help to know that these stages of grief are normal? In what ways are you asking, "Why, God?" Describe how a "Why, God?" makes you feel. How does Jesus feel about the ways in which you hurt? How do you know? See the shortest verse in the Bible, John 11:35.

4. How would you describe denial? Why can the numbness of disbelief be the Lord's kindness? How could your continuing denial of what is happening be harmful if you did not leave that stage behind?

5. Joe Bayly's "A Psalm on the Death of an 18-year-old Son" is extremely honest. Do you think he would have written that kind of poem if he knew it was going to be published? Why or why not?

6. In the anger of grief we may lash out at someone who is completely innocent but happened to cross our path at the wrong time. Explain how anger can increase our hurt and loneliness.

7. Make a list of ways you feel God has given you a bum deal. In what ways do you want to turn away from God because you feel angry?

8. What is the difference between God's correction and the suffering of illness? Give examples of ways we might bargain with God when we are suffering. Do you think God understands how you feel? Why or why not?

9. Return to Romans 8:28. As you think more about it, what does that passage mean to you? In what ways have you turned toward God in spite of your anger? Make a second list, this one of the ways God has brought good out of something painful in your life.

10. What is the difference between habitual grumbling and an honest cry of pain to God?

11. Have you offered some really honest prayers to him? Did you drop dead afterwards? How did he help you deal with your feelings and the situation involved? Describe how he used your honesty to give healing.

12. As Jesus died on the cross he cried out, "My God, my God, why have you forsaken me?" (Mark 15:33 NIV). Why do you think that could have been the most difficult moment in his suffering? What does it tell you about his willingness to die for each of us?

13. What does it mean to say that Jesus weeps with us? Give examples of times when God reached out to give you new experiences in grace and a new sense of his love.

To pray about:

> *Thank God that you can be honest with him. Ask him to help you sense his presence in spite of all that is happening to you.*

Session 4: Plug into Power

Chapter 7: Prayer That Makes a Difference

1. *Read Luke 11:1-4.* When his disciples saw Jesus praying, it was so appealing to them that they asked, "Lord, teach us to pray."

2. Why does prayer hold the key for the most important relationship any one of us can ever have? How does the word *childlike* express what that relationship can be? Think of other words that describe your relationship in prayer. List them.

3. Whenever Jesus spoke of his Father, it was clear that they had a relationship. "He who has seen me has seen the Father," he told Philip. "Do you not believe that I am in the Father and the Father in me? The words that I say to you I do not speak on my own authority; but the Father who dwells in me does his works" (John 14:9-10). On another occasion he told the Jews, "My teaching is not mine, but his who sent me" (John 7:16). What

did Jesus do in order to keep his relationship with the Father in good repair? How can you keep your relationship with Jesus in good repair?

4. Jesus also explains his ability to perform miracles. See John 10:30, 37-38. Have you experienced a miracle. Tell about it.

5. Why should you pray when God knows everything about you? For just a few of the great prayer promises, read Matthew 7:7-8; John 15:7-8; Mark 11:24; and Matthew 18:18-20. What is the difference between Christ *inviting* us to pray and *commanding* that we should? Which does Jesus do?

6. What if your prayers don't seem to have the power that you want? Read Psalm 66:18; 51; and Matthew 7:7-9. What does it mean to ask, seek, knock?

7. Do you need to have good feelings when you pray? Why or why not? Does your faith have to be 100 percent there? How do you know? Check out Matthew 17:20.

8. In his time of suffering, Job came to a revelation about who God is (Job 42:5). How do you think Job felt about praying for the "friends" who made him feel even worse about the disasters he faced? Yet what happened when Job prayed for these friends? See Job 42:7-17.

9. An easy guide for keeping our prayer relationship in balance is found in the acronym ACTS: Adoration, Confession, Thanksgiving, Supplication. Talk about the meaning of each of these words. If needed, use your dictionary to define the word *supplication*.

10. Sniveling. What is it? Why is it important to tell God *specific* needs and ask in an attitude of thanksgiving and praise? When is a prayer request too small? When is a request too big? Explain.

11. God has promised to supply our needs, but not our wants. What is the difference? At the same time, God goes far beyond supplying our needs. Give examples from your own experience.

If your study group runs out of time, this would be a good stopping point. Otherwise, continue.

12. What does it mean to explain away an answer to prayer? What is a more positive approach that cheers the heart of God?

13. Many of the prayer promises are conditional. If you take care of the condition, the promise follows. Read John 15:7. What is the condition for receiving whatever you ask?

14. How does a healthy human relationship guide you in what you ask? How does your relationship with God also guide you?

15. As you pray, you may *give up* on something or *give it over* to the Lord. What is the difference? What does it mean to let God carry the weight of something that concerns you? Tell about times when he helped you cope with something difficult. Have those times come when you've chosen to begin praising him, even with tears running down your cheeks?

16. Think about other times when you haven't been able to give a weight over to the Lord. Return to chapter 2, page 12, for a practical way to turn something over to the Lord. What do you want to do with your suitcase?

17. Who gives the power for your prayers? Why is the name of Jesus so important?

18. Why do you need authority in prayer? If you desire more authority in your prayer life, how can you receive it?

19. When you intercede for someone, what are you actually doing? Can you begin to guess what the throne room of heaven must be like? Give your ideas; then turn to Ephesians 1:17-23. If all things are under the feet of Jesus, what authority does he have over what happens in prayer?

20. Near the end of his earthly life, Jesus looked toward heaven and prayed for himself, then for his disciples and all believers. Read John 17:1-5 NIV to see the authority given him by the Father. For the authority of the Holy Spirit, see John 16:13.

21. A position in Christ is more than an attitude. Think about a hard-fought football game or a painful war between two countries or people groups. What happens with the front lines? What do you think it means to gain a position in prayer?

22. Set aside a place in the notebook you use as a prayer journal to list references and write out the words of prayer promises you find in the Bible. In your daily devotions, keep adding to that gold

mine. Return to those promises often. What do you suppose will happen to your faith? Your authority in prayer?

If authority in prayer is dependent on your relationship with Jesus, what does it tell you about your need to grow deeper in knowing him?

To pray about:
> *Take extra time to pray together as a group. Ask for the authority of Jesus in your prayers.*

Session 5: Reach for Healing

Chapter 8: God's Remedy for Pain

The woman was sure of one thing. "I can't forgive him," she said. "What's more, I *won't* forgive him." Her shoulders hunched over, her eyes dark and deep with pain, she seemed to be withdrawing from the world.

1. *Read John 19:1-24; and Luke 23:34:* When Jesus died for us, he provided the way by which our sins are forgiven. He also showed us how to forgive others. Can you hear his cry from the cross— "Father, forgive them; for they know not what they do"? What does that cry tell you about Jesus? How does it help you see him in a deeper way?

2. If you forgive someone who hurt you, does it mean you're saying that what that person did was right?

3. Where have you found the word *cancer* in the Bible? What illness shown in the Bible might be a social parallel? In the time of Jesus, how were people with that illness treated by others? What were these people expected to do? See Luke 17:11-19. When you read how they were healed, what does it do for your faith?

4. *Read Matthew 6:12-15:* What condition is attached to the promise of our being forgiven?

5. Is it necessary to have good feelings about a person in order to forgive? What does it mean to choose to forgive? Why does forgiveness become God's remedy for pain?

6. If you forgive with your will, what happens with your emotions? Does it always happen immediately? How do you know?

7. During marital counseling, Lois's father often told couples, "Before you go to bed at night, either come to agreement or agree to disagree. That way you'll always be in agreement." Why does this guideline have the potential to change your entire life?

8. Try it another way: "Do not let the sun go down on your wrath." How can this idea be helpful in every relationship?

9. What are some words you can use in attempting reconciliation with another person? What if someone does not respond to your attempts at reconciliation? See Romans 12:17-21.

To pray about:
Choose to get rid of the leftover baggage in your life.

Chapter 9: Words That Give Us Life

1. *Read John 20:19-23* in different versions and paraphrases: In the RSV, verse 23 reads, "If you forgive the sins of any, they are forgiven; if you retain the sins of any, they are retained." How are unforgiven sins retained? What happens to the person retaining or holding in the hurt and consequences of someone else's sin?

2. Write the words of the John 20:23 prayer in your prayer journal. Let the words sink deep into your spirit. Highlight them so you can return to that prayer whenever needed. Then think about how you can use that prayer right now. Why is it important to pray in the name of Jesus?

3. What part does your free will play in whether you receive healing? How many times do you need to offer the John 20:23 prayer before God hears you? How do you know?

4. If someone has angered you at work, how can you change the pattern of what is happening? If someone in your personal relationships has wounded you deeply, what can you do about it? Study the steps involved in the "Take Responsibility," "Change the Pattern," and "Forgive and Forget?" sections. How can you take responsibility for your healing? What part does God play? What part do you play?

5. *Read Matthew 18:21-25:* How many times do we need to forgive? Give reasons for your answer. Does this passage mean we are to accept or live with physical abuse? Why or why not?

6. Why is it sometimes necessary to sacrifice your desire to win? Which is more important, winning a battle or winning the war? Explain your thinking.

7. For a word of comfort remember this: If the person you need to forgive has died, Jesus still hears your prayer. Just pray it!

To pray about:
> Ask Jesus to show you the people you need to forgive. Then pray in his name, forgiving those people.

Session 6: Discover God's Message

Chapter 10: You Can Hear the Voice of God

1. *Read Exodus 33:12-23:* Why did Moses need to know that God's presence was with him? Glance back to Exodus 32 and Exodus 33:1-11. What did God tell Moses in order to reassure him? In what ways do you need to hear God say, "I will give you rest"?

2. *Read 1 Kings 19:1-13:* Give at least two reasons why Elijah needed to hear the voice of God. What similar reasons do you have in your own life? Does the phrase *hearing the voice of God* refer to an actual voice? Explain.

3. What are two important ways in which you can hear the voice of God? How can you hear God's voice through Scripture? With each means of guidance, list the guidelines and checkpoints that help you understand what he is saying.

4. What does it mean to receive "inward assurance"? Name some of the ways by which you might receive that assurance of God's leading. How can you recognize the inner knowing or "I ought to" feeling that is God's leading, not outward pressure? Has God ever spoken to you through a dream or a vision? Describe what happened. What spiritual insight did you receive?

To pray about:
  Praise Jesus for his presence in your life.

Chapter 11: Going Beyond Confusion

1. *Read 1 Samuel 19:1-10; and 20:1-17:* What is the unenviable position in which Jonathan lived? What does it mean to say that Jonathan knew the mind of God?

2. Under God's gracious leading, confusion offers the potential for certainty in him. Name some specific ways God gives to help us go beyond confusion. How has his leading made a difference in your life? Think of a time when he helped you with something you needed to know. Describe what he did. How did things fall into place?

3. The Bible tells us that when Ruth lost her husband through death, she was childless and could have stayed in her own country. Instead she helped her mother-in-law Naomi by walking with her to Bethlehem. As Ruth went out to earn a living for both of them, "she happened to come to the portion of field belonging to Boaz" (Ruth 2:3 NAS). When Christians use the word *happened,* as in "She just happened to be in the right place at the right time," what do they mean?

4. What is a God-planned coincidence? Have there been times when you have explained away such "coincidences" in your own life? What happened when you said, "Oh, that was just a coincidence"? If, instead, you thanked God for his answer, what happened to your level of faith? How do you account for the difference? How do you think the Holy Spirit feels about your giving thanks?

5. Name some possible confirming circumstances. What does it mean to "test the waters"? What is one means of guidance that cannot be imitated by anyone or anything? Give examples from your own life.

6. There's a stop, look, and listen in 1 Corinthians 14:33. Describe a practical way in which you can use that verse.

7. If you outline chapters 11 and 12, you'll have a quick reference guide for hearing the voice of God. Every once in a while,

return to these chapters and see how God shows you new evidence of his leading as you continue to grow in him.

To pray about:
> Thank Jesus for the leading he has already given you. Ask for his ability to continue growing in the way you recognize his voice.

Session 7: Receive the Healing of Jesus

Chapter 12: God's Provision for Wholeness

1. *Read John 9:1-33:* What was the blind man's statement of faith about what Jesus had done for him? Why does his testimony increase your faith? Continue to study the life principles given in each chapter. You may want to memorize the "Faith Thought" verses.

2. How would you define wholeness? What are some ways that prayers for physical wholeness are answered? Have you received physical healing? Tell about it, giving the honor to Jesus.

3. What is spiritual and emotional wholeness? Give examples from your own life or the lives of people you know.

4. Which is most important to you, spiritual, emotional, intellectual, or physical healing? Why? Explain the reasons for your answer.

5. When God gives a special word to you, you are not cranking up some emotional high. Rather, you sense that message from him as something spontaneous and real. In what way have you received a healing message from Jesus? Are there ways in which you have received wholeness but not physical healing?

To pray about:
> Seek Jesus about any areas of healing in which you need his help.

Chapter 13: Making Christianity Practical

1. *Read Acts 3:1-16:* How can you make Christianity practical in your own life? In the life of someone else? In what ways can

prayer for healing become a team effort? Explain why that is important. Consider the most important factor of all. In whose name do you pray? Read on through Acts 4:31. Memorize such verses as Acts 3:6, 16; and 4:19-20, 29-30.

2. If you received a life-threatening diagnosis of cancer, how would you want people to pray? How would you feel if their prayers for physical healing *weren't* answered?

3. What are the steps in praying for divine healing? What are some safeguards in how we support the medical profession in our prayers for healing?

4. In what ways can you walk alongside people living with life-threatening illnesses or long-term, difficult situations? How important is the faith of a patient? Give reasons for your answer.

5. What is meant by "ultimate" healing or healing where "more of the life of God enters into a person"?

6. Why is it important to sense when it's someone's time to die? How does it make a difference in the way you pray?

7. What does it mean to "lose" a healing? What steps can be taken to "keep" God's sovereign healing? (This is not a denial of reality to force something that isn't there. Rather, it is keeping the enemy from stealing a gift.) Name important factors for standing in faith for God's healing once it has occurred.

To pray about:
As you pray for healing for others or yourself, ask Jesus to give you gifts of faith.

Chapter 14: Healing from the Inside Out

1. Lay hold of Jeremiah 30:17: "'For I will restore health to you, and your wounds I will heal,' says the Lord." Name some of the ways in which you have experienced loss in your life. What does it mean to be healed "from the inside out?" Is that kind of healing something you need? Why?

2. What does it mean to have our pain understood by those who hold it with gentle hands? How does sharing a grief with an understanding person help your friendship grow?

3. How do you view yourself? If you have a negative view of yourself, what reasons can you give for why that has happened? If you need to deal with those experiences, why can "Yes, but . . ." be an excuse? How does the feeling of being loved differ from the knowledge of being loved? Explain. Give examples from your own life.

4. How do you think God sees you? Why do you hold that belief? Can you support your belief through a verse or verses in Scripture? Let's take one of the most special Bible verses—John 3:16: "For God so loved the world that he gave his only Son, that whoever believes in him should not perish but have eternal life." *Whoever*. Who does that include?

5. The forgiveness of your sin is a necessary foundation for your self-esteem. If there is a sin separating you from God, be sorry about it. Ask his forgiveness. Then receive the mind-boggling promise of 2 Corinthians 5:17. What does that verse tell you about who you are if you have made your peace with Jesus?

6. Sort out some other issues: What is your perception of success? Your attitude about real happiness? What expectations do you have for yourself? What expectations do you believe God has for you? Do you believe your expectations for yourself are the same as God's expectations for you? Why or why not?

7. If you look to God instead of comparing yourself with others, what do you find? How does God see you? Check out Psalm 139:13-16a; Romans 5:8; Psalm 103:10-12; Deuteronomy 1:29-31; Psalm 84:1 (You *are* the dwelling place of the Lord!); and Psalm 45:11 NIV.

8. *Read Mark 14:1-9:* From John's gospel we know that this was Mary, the sister of Martha and Lazarus. Anointing with oil was a common occurrence at feasts in Jesus' day (Ps. 23:5; Luke 7:46). Why is it important that you show your deep devotion to Jesus? What do you suppose it means to him?

To pray about:
Choose to worship Jesus for who he is.

Session 8: Be Re-Created!

Chapter 15: Lonesome for Home

1. *Read John 14:1-6:* What home has Jesus prepared for us? How do you know? What does it mean to be lonesome for home?

2. In what ways might it be necessary to relinquish a loved one?

3. What are some of the gifts Lois received from the people whose homegoing she shared? What special gifts have you received from loved ones? What special gifts are you offering to others, even now?

4. What is an Old Testament kind of blessing? Read examples from Scripture: Genesis 48–49; and Deuteronomy 33.

5. If you could choose the illness by which you would die, what would it be? Why? What are some benefits in dying that way?

6. Think about Philippians 3:7-11. In what ways can we help our loved ones deal with the separation of death—our own or that of someone else?

To pray about:

Thank God for the way he has used the special people in your life. Cherish the moments you have enjoyed forever.

Chapter 16: The Season of Singing

1. Remember Moses? How he changed from being the stepson of Pharaoh's daughter to a lonely shepherd? Tell how the Lord has used your time of suffering. Stand back enough to see the ways he has begun to re-create you. How has he increased your love for and appreciation of him? Describe your newfound understandings.

2. List the ways the Lord has given your life back to you. How has he changed your attitudes for the rest of your time on earth? In what ways has he released power in your life? In what ways would you like to receive even more of this power of the Holy Spirit?

3. *Read Mark 6:6b-13:* When Jesus sent out his disciples he said, "Take nothing for the journey except a staff—no bread, no bag,

no money in your belts. Wear sandals, but not an extra tunic." The disciples went out from village to village, preaching the gospel and healing the sick.

A seasoned traveler lightens his or her luggage in every way possible. In what ways has your experience of suffering stripped you of extra baggage?

4. If you have left your extra baggage behind, God can use you. When you look to Jesus in every circumstance, he sets you free to serve. You have seen his glory. You join his disciples in saying, "We cannot but speak of what we have seen and heard" (Acts 4:20).

Unless you're an artist and can do better, draw a stick figure of yourself in the center of a piece of paper. Around that figure write the names of people with whom you have your closest personal relationships. Draw a circle around the stick figure and names. Mark that circle number 1.

As though you were making a bull's eye, draw three other circles around the first one. Moving out from the center, number the circles 2, 3, and 4. In circle 2 write the names of people you see frequently in work, community, medical, or church contexts. In circle 3 write the names of people you see less often and on a random basis. Include in this circle the names of occupations that touch your life, but for whom you may not have a person's name. The bus or taxi driver, for instance. A flight attendant, receptionist, nurse, librarian, or the servers in a restaurant you frequent.

You may have trouble deciding whether someone belongs in circle 2 or 3. A person who enters your life in the third sphere may move closer to the center as you become better acquainted. Do the best you can to re-create your world, but don't be concerned about having an absolutely precise drawing.

These ever-widening circles represent the spheres of your life. Outside circle 3, leave the outer edge open. This is a sphere without boundaries. Name areas of your own country or distant places for which you'd like to pray. Think big. Dream strong.

5. Look at your drawing. Think about the people involved, the lives you touch in one way or another. If you are part of a study

group, compare your drawing with that of others. What is your basic sphere of ministry? For what people are you most responsible in terms of prayer and feeding into someone's life? Why can your circle become as big as you want to make it?

6. Now change that image of a bull's eye into something else. Remember what it's like to throw a stone into a pond? Consider how your influence for Jesus can move out in ever-widening circles. In what specific ways can you—by the power and leading of the Holy Spirit—start a ripple that continues to widen?

7. With the leading of the Spirit of Jesus, set a goal for yourself. Tell God about it. Perhaps you'd like to use the words of Romans 14:7-8: "None of us lives to himself only, none of us dies for himself only. If we live, it is for the Lord that we live, and if we die, it is for the Lord that we die. So whether we live or die, we belong to the Lord."

Either way, you win. Either way, I win. Now enter the Lord's season of singing!

To pray about:

Ask Jesus to release in and through you all the power you need to witness and live your daily life in him.

WORKS
REFERENCED

———————◆●◆———————

Barclay, William. *The Promise of the Spirit*. Philadelphia: Westminster Press/ Epworth Press, 1960.

Bayly, Joseph. *View from a Hearse: A Christian View of Death*. Elgin, Ill.: David C. Cook, 1969.

———. "A Psalm on the death of an 18-year-old son." In *Psalms of My Life*. Colorado Springs: Victor Books, 2000.

Bittner, Vernon. *Make Your Illness Count*. Minneapolis, Minn.: Augsburg, 1976.

Chambers, Oswald. *My Utmost for His Highest*. Edited by James Reimann. Grand Rapids, Mich.: Discovery House, 1992.

Chant, Ken. Retreat for spiritual leaders, Cambridge, Minn., date unknown.

Erdahl, Lowell, and Carol Erdahl. *Be Good to Each Other: An Open Letter on Marriage*. Minneapolis, Minn.: Augsburg, 1991.

Evenson, Leland. Sermon at Vision of Glory Lutheran Church, Plymouth, Minn., date unknown.

Foss, Michael W. Sermon at Prince of Peace Lutheran Church, Burnsville, Minn., February 16, 1997.

Frost, Gerhard. *Bless My Growing*. Minneapolis, Minn.: Augsburg, 1974.

Gilliland, Pat. "Christians, Jews Plan Tabernacle Near Bomb Site." *Daily Oklahoman* (June 21, 1995): 1–2.

Hallesby, O. *Prayer*. Minneapolis, Minn.: Augsburg, 1959.

Hanson, Richard Simon. "Real Forgiveness." *Lutheran Standard* (November 19, 1982): 4–7.

Johnson, Lois Walfrid. *The Fiddler's Secret*. Minneapolis, Minn.: Bethany House, 1998.

———. *Gift in My Arms: Thoughts for New Mothers*. Minneapolis, Minn.: Augsburg, 1977.

Keller, Philip. *A Shepherd Looks at Psalm 23.* Grand Rapids, Mich.: Zondervan, 1970.

————. *A Shepherd Looks at the Good Shepherd and His Sheep.* Grand Rapids, Mich.: Zondervan, 1978.

Kennedy, Rose Fitzgerald. *Times to Remember.* New York: Doubleday, 1974.

Klobuchar, Jim. Column. Minneapolis *Star* (September 4, 1970).

Kübler-Ross, Elisabeth. *On Death and Dying.* New York: Macmillan, 1969.

Lewis, C. S. *A Grief Observed.* New York: Seabury Press, 1961.

————. *Mere Christianity.* New York: Macmillan, 1952.

MacNutt, Francis. *The Power to Heal.* Notre Dame, Ind.: Ave Maria Press, 1977.

Murray, Andrew. *With Christ in the School of Prayer.* Old Tappan, N.J.: Fleming H. Revell, 1953.

Peterman, Mary. *Healing: A Spiritual Adventure.* Philadelphia: Fortress Press, 1974.

Rogness, Alvin N. *Appointment with God: Bible Study Resource Book.* Minneapolis, Minn.: Augsburg, 1978.

————. *The Wonder of Being Loved.* Minneapolis, Minn.: Augsburg, 1972.

Shakespeare, William. *Julius Caesar.* Act 2, scene 2, line 32.

Sherrill, John. "My Friend, the Bible." *Guideposts* (November 1978).

Taylor, Dr. and Mrs. Howard. *Hudson Taylor and the China Inland Mission: The Growth of a Work of God.* London: China Inland Mission, 1918.

ten Boom, Corrie, with John Sherrill and Elizabeth Sherrill. *The Hiding Place.* Chappaqua, N.Y.: Chosen Books, 1971.

Tuttle, Robert C., Jr. *Face to Face* (February 1973): 26–27.

Vossler, Bill. "How to Age Well." *Bond* (March/April 2000): 18–21.

Wilkerson, David. Sermon, Times Square Church Pulpit Series, Manhattan, N.Y., and World Challenge, Lindale, Texas, date unknown.

ACKNOWLEDGMENTS

FEW BOOKS ARE THE PRODUCT OF A SINGLE PERSON, and that's especially true with this one. Born of a request by editor Roger Palms of *Decision* magazine, the original story of what happened to me was published in several countries and languages and reprinted in the *Bond*, *The Lutheran Standard,* and *Sunday Digest.* Yet not one word would have been written without the prayers of countless people throughout the world.

Special thanks to Mark Hillmer, from whom I was taking a seminary class when I was diagnosed with cancer. Thanks to Dick Blank, who joined Mark in praying for me, as well as countless other pastors and friends along the way. Thanks to Betsy Anderson, Bruce Cameron, Vern Bittner, Joe Bayly, Bill Young, David Sorensen, Charlotte Adelsperger, my critique group, the Saturday Club, Dick Weekley, Charette Barta, and Kristi Smith.

My love to those within my family who have suffered because of physical cancer, as well as to patients and their families everywhere. Thanks to those who have suffered from other forms of cancer and shared their stories and their lives with me. Ours is a partnership of asking questions about truths that are eternal.

Thanks to Bob Moluf and Roland Seboldt, the original editors of *Either Way, I Win;* to those who worked on this updated edition, Ron Klug and Martha Rosenquist; and to the entire Augsburg Fortress team.

Finally, my gratitude to my husband, Roy, for understanding my pain and holding it with gentle hands. Thanks to our children—Gail Swanson, Jeff Johnson, and Kevin Johnson—and their families for supporting us in our time of need.

Finally, and most important, thank you to my Lord Jesus Christ, who died that I might live. Because of him I can boldly proclaim, "Either way, I win!"

BOOKS BY LOIS WALFRID JOHNSON

Picture books
Aaron's Christmas Donkey
Hello, God!

Young Readers Series
Just a Minute, Lord
You're My Best Friend, Lord

**Let's-Talk-About-It Stories
for Kids**
You're Worth More Than You Think!
Secrets of the Best Choice
You Are Wonderfully Made!
Thanks for Being My Friend

**Adventures
of the Northwoods**
The Disappearing Stranger
The Hidden Message
The Creeping Shadows
The Vanishing Footprints
Trouble at Wild River

The Mysterious Hideaway
Grandpa's Stolen Treasure
The Runaway Clown
Mystery of the Missing Map
Disaster on Windy Hill

The Riverboat Adventures
Escape into the Night
Race for Freedom
Midnight Rescue
The Swindler's Treasure
Mysterious Signal
The Fiddler's Secret

Young Teens Series
Come as You Are

Adult books
Gift in My Arms
Either Way, I Win
Songs for Silent Moments
Falling Apart or Coming Together

CPSIA information can be obtained at www.ICGtesting.com
Printed in the USA
LVOW011011251111

256352LV00004B/40/A